HELPING ADOLESCENTS IN SCHOOL

Tony Branwhite

Westport, Connecticut
London

Library of Congress Cataloging-in-Publication Data

Branwhite, Tony.
  Helping adolescents in school / Tony Branwhite.
      p.   cm.
  Includes bibliographical references and index.
  ISBN 0–275–96898–7 (alk. paper)
  1. School psychology.   2. Adolescent psychology.   I. Title.
LB1027.55.B72   2000
  155.5—dc21   99–086104

British Library Cataloguing in Publication Data is available.

Library of Congress Catalog Card Number: 99–086104
ISBN: 0–275–96898–7

First published in 2000

Praeger Publishers, 88 Post Road West, Westport, CT 06881
An imprint of Greenwood Publishing Group, Inc.
www.praeger.com

Printed in the United States of America

*This book is dedicated to those caring professionals
who are willing to learn from young people
and committed to providing them
with excellent personal support in school*

Contents

Figures

Acknowledgments

The inspiration for writing this book came, like the headwaters of a river, from several different sources. In particular, however, I would like to thank the many young people, teachers, parents, and colleagues who have taught me things that I might otherwise have missed completely. Some of the insights that they felt able to share with me came from hard-won experience, and this helped me to realize that none of us holds the full deck of cards when trying to understanding the adolescent experience.

Many researchers readily responded to requests for information from me, a complete stranger. Their generosity in helping me to gain greater awareness of significant developments in the field is a kindness for which I am deeply grateful. Also, my editor, Nita Romer, and producer, John Beck, stimulated more rapid action on my part than might otherwise have been the case.

Last, but not least, my wife Jo was able to contend with my need to disappear frequently and write into the wee hours and kindly tolerated lapses of attention in the middle of normal conversation, while I fell momentarily into thinking about some current aspect of the manuscript. Perhaps this book was unwittingly a labor of love for both of us!

1

Contemporary Issues

Adult's views of teenagers often tend to extremes. Some regard the teenage years as halcyon times; a period in life free from "real worries." At the other extreme there is a pervasive anti-youth feeling, fuelled perhaps by the media, which paints the teenager as hedonistic and unruly with a casual disrespect for both people and property.

Gordon & Grant 1997, 1–2

PART ONE:
KEY CONCEPTS IN THE STUDY OF ADOLESCENCE

Defining Adolescence

The term adolescence is derived from the Latin verb "adolescere," meaning "to grow to maturity." In keeping with that view, Hastin-Bennett (1993) defines adolescence as the period between puberty and the end of bodily growth. From this perspective, adolescence is held to be the time when a child reaches biological maturity. However, the same writer also asserts that rapid physiological change may produce difficulties in psychological development leading to turbulent behavior. It is further suggested that adolescence may produce particular difficulty for parents, who may have to call on all their reserves of tolerance and understanding. Although this proposal links physiological and psychological change, it remains in some respects unsatisfactory, because it goes beyond the central task of defining adolescence.

An alternative approach may be to set the limits of adolescence by ruling out the preceding and following stages of development. Herbert (1994) suggests that we have clear notions of childhood and adulthood, in that children are wholly dependent upon their parents for love, nurturance, and guidance, while adults are required to be independent and able to care for themselves. We might therefore think of adolescence as a period between dependence and independence, bridging childhood and adulthood, and this type of definition (adolescence as an intervening period) is similar to that favored by the *Concise Oxford English Dictionary*. Burningham (1994) also advances a view which is compatible with this standpoint by suggesting that adolescence is a transitional period occurring between the dependency of childhood and the responsibilities of adult life.

Herbert adopts a different emphasis in defining adolescence, which reaches beyond biology by arguing that adolescence refers particularly to psychological developments, although these are broadly related to the physical growth processes indicated by the term "puberty." This view is reinforced by Reber (1985) who marks the beginning of adolescence by the onset of puberty, but who identifies its end with the attainment of both physiological and psychological maturity. Yet, insofar as those psychological changes leading to maturity may not be completed within the adolescent period, that definition likewise has some constraints. Although the onset of puberty marks the beginning of the adolescent period, it seems likely to be cultural and socioeconomic considerations rather than biological factors that mark its ending (Muus 1975). Reber also notes that the term adolescence lacks precision, arguing that both the onset of puberty and the attainment of maturity are impossible to specify.

Perhaps it is shortcomings such as these that have lead to the adoption of alternative approaches to the definition of adolescence. For example, Petersen (1988) observes that schools emphasize the importance of chronological age, virtually regardless of developmental status. Therefore Petersen places emphasis upon the second decade of life as defining the adolescent period. However, those at the end of their second decade are likely to have left school and moreover may not wish to identify themselves with the adolescent label. Accordingly, other options may be more appropriate, and one further possibility is to take legal concepts into account. In English law the age of majority is attained at eighteen years of age, and therefore a pragmatic alternative is to view adolescence as a period of development extending from puberty to the age of eighteen. One advantage of this approach is that it eliminates much of the difficulty implicit in dealing with different thresholds for physical and psychological maturity. Accordingly, it will provide the definition of adolescence generally adopted in this text.

Psychology and Adolescence

While the earliest beginnings of adult interest in the development and well-being of young people are difficult to identify, the start of the scientific study of adolescence by psychologists can be determined with pinpoint accuracy. In 1904, G. Stanley Hall, president of Clark University and founder of the American Psychological Association, published a two-volume study entitled *Adolescence: Its Psychology and its Relations to Physiology, Anthropology, Sociology, Sex, Crime, Religion and Education.* In the course of this monumental work, Hall characterized adolescence in sweeping terms:

Adolescence is a new birth, for the higher and more completely human traits are now born. The qualities of body and soul that now emerge are far newer. The child comes from and harks back to a remoter past; the adolescent is neo-atavistic, and in him the later acquisitions of race slowly become prepotent. Development is less gradual and more saltatory, suggestive of some ancient period of storm and stress when old moorings were broken and a higher level attained. (1904, xiii)

According to Conger and Petersen (1984) many subsequent writers have been influenced by Hall's recapitulation theory of development, viewing his work as a one-sided exponent of a strictly biological, maturational concept of adolescence, one which ignored the effects of culture. Such an interpretation, they suggest, could be erroneous. In fact, Hall draws a clear distinction between the role of biological and environmental factors during adolescence, stating that "young children grow despite great hardships, but later adolescence is more dependent upon favouring conditions in the environment, disturbances of which more readily cause arrest and prevent maturity" (1904, 47).

Hence it appears that Hall actually suggested an increase in the influence of environmental factors during adolescence. The long-term importance, however, of Hall's contribution is probably to be found less in his recapitulation theory than it is in his establishment of adolescence as a distinctive field of psychological investigation. This single-handed achievement stimulated a great deal of subsequent professional interest that today supports several journals devoted exclusively to the study of adolescence. Hence adolescent psychology has come of age as a largely natural (ecological) science rather than an experimental one, given that much of the material included is based upon observational data (Ansubel, Montmeyor, & Svajian 1977).

Models of Adolescence

Despite significant progress in the field, opinion regarding the interpretation of psychological research on adolescent development diverges, and therefore a brief discussion of the two main models of adolescence seems warranted at this point.

Adolescence As Disturbed Development

A number of later researchers, perhaps influenced by Hall's use of the phrase "storm and stress," imply that adolescence is an acute phase of human development. For example, Copeland and Hess (1995) refer to adolescence as a *crucial* time in the development of the individual, and Fitzgerald, Joseph, Hayes, and O'Regan (1995) suggest that it is no less than a *critical* period for the formation of attitudes toward life (author's italics). The use of terms like crucial or critical suggests that these writers construe the adolescent years as exercising particularly powerful effects upon the development of the individual. In promoting this model, certain authors have added somewhat paradoxical observations. Hutter (1938) for example remarks that adolescence is abnormal if everything passes normally, and Hyatt-Williams (1975) concludes that adolescence without normative crisis is not adolescence.

These suggestions by no means exhaust the range of concerns which have been expressed about development during adolescence. Reference to some form of conflict seems to occur in the work of many authorities. For instance, Friedenberg (1959) has characterized adolescence as a protracted conflict between the individual and society. More recently, Herbert (1989) infers that adolescents are often rightly thought of as disciplinary headaches for their parents. Mussen, Conger, and Kagan (1970) assert that some alarmed observers believe that young people have become more rebellious, more troubled emotionally, more promiscuous sexually, less idealistic, more critical of the values and standards of adult culture, and more disengaged from them.

Eastman and Rosen (1994) go so far as to assert that the teenage years can be shattering times. The most easygoing teenagers, they suggest, feel overwhelmed at times, and find that the balancing act of juggling feelings, responsibilities, and the needs of others can sometimes seem like just too much to cope with. This notion may not be entirely without foundation, since Rutter (1977) refers to the discovery that inner turmoil, as represented by feelings of misery, self-deprecation, and ideas of being laughed at, are at least common among early adolescents.

Other writers have taken the position that adolescence actually represents some form of psychopathology. Notably, Freud (1953) asserts that during adolescence the sexual impulses break through to produce the subordination of all sexual components—instincts under the primacy of the genital zone. From psychoanalytic theory, this predicts that the adolescent will attempt to resolve earlier Oedipal conflicts, a goal which is achieved in part by transferring individual attachments to new relationships. Anna Freud (1950) offers the opinion that adolescent manifestations come close to symptom formation of neurotic, psychotic, or dissocial order, and merge almost imperceptibly into almost all of the mental illnesses. Kretschmer (1951) implies that adolescence is a period of human development which generates an increase in schizoid characteristics. From the same psychoanalytic tradition, Von Krevelin (1970; cited in Herbert 1994, 195) suggests that adolescence is a period of life which by its disintegrative character may seem like a psychosis itself.

While these views have been widely disseminated, however, Douvan and Adelson (1966) concluded from a large-scale study that the traditional psychoanalytic view was based upon sensitive, articulate, middle-class adolescents. Since they may not represent the broad range of characteristics in the wider adolescent population, this research team argues that the validity of the conclusions drawn must therefore be limited accordingly.

Adolescence As Normal Development

Working within a different research paradigm, it was the anthropologist Margaret Mead (1961) who posed the timely question of whether mental and emotional distress during adolescence is as inevitable as teething is a period of misery for the small baby. In answer to that question, there is now a sufficient number of published opinions to support an alternate view, namely that adolescence should be regarded as a period of normal functioning. However, within this framework, Boldero and Fallon (1995) have concluded that adolescence is a period which involves change in several important dimensions, and Coleman (1989) refers to adolescence as a developmental stage associated with a number of problems, although he does not imply that this is a causal association.

Taking a broad view, Hilgard and Atkinson (1967) describe the adolescent period as only a phase in the stream of human growth. They also argue that it is a mistake to emphasize too sharply any discontinuities in comparison with other phases of human growth. In keeping with this opinion, a four-year follow-up study of children living on the Isle of Wight (Graham & Rutter 1973) suggested that psychiatric disorders were only slightly more common at fourteen and fifteen than they had been at ten and eleven. With comparable restraint, Nurmi, Poole, and Kalakoski (1994) conceptualize adolescence as a transitional period of personality development which can incorporate a period of thinking about the future. Steinberg and Silverberg (1986) also contend that emotional autonomy and self-reliance increase during the adolescent years. Likewise, Blos (1979) suggests that adolescence is a time of renegotiating relationships with parents, a process which requires cognitive and interpersonal competence. After reviewing several normative studies of teenage relationships, Lewis (1993) has also argued in favor of a developmentally evolving capacity for intimacy and relatedness during the adolescent years.

Another carefully considered opinion is provided by Conger and Petersen (1984). These writers note that while many adolescents feel occasional periods of uncertainty and self-doubt, of loneliness and sadness, or of anxiety and concern for the future, they are also likely to experience joy, excitement, curiosity, a sense of adventure, and a feeling of competence in mastering new challenges. Conger and Petersen also remark that although a high degree of emotional turmoil characterizes some adolescents, there has been an unwarranted tendency on the part of some clinicians to generalize too readily to the average adolescent findings obtained from a limited segment of the population. Further qualification is provided by Fontana (1991). This author provides an interactionist perspective on the relationship between adolescence and challenging behavior, in which he asserts that it is not physiological changes that create rebellious teenagers, but society itself, through its artificial methods of relating to young people. One form which this takes in a complex industrial society, he suggests, is keeping the young in a subservient role (i.e., still attending school) long after they have reached physical maturity.

Whatever the quality of their experience, in the view of Havinghurst (1952) during early to mid-adolescence, young people have a series of developmental tasks to accomplish. Over forty years later, Nurmi, Poole, and Kalakoski (1994) have proposed a contemporary version of this earlier suggestion. The tasks specified include achieving mature relationships with peers, forming a sex-role identity, achieving emotional independence from parents, planning educational goals, preparing for an economic career, and becoming orientated for marriage and adult family life. The development of such ideas reflects professional assumptions that adolescent change should usually be perceived as normal human development.

While Mussen, Conger, and Kagan (1970) suggest there is general agreement that the adolescent period presents special adjustment problems, none of the above authors imply that adolescence causes pathological functioning. Significantly, nonclinic studies of adolescents (see for example Grinker and Werble 1974; and Offer and Offer 1975) found that most adolescents were reasonably well adjusted.

This seems to be a recurrent finding, since Offer and Schonert-Reichl (1992) indicate that the majority of recent research suggests that adolescence should not be represented as a time of severe emotional upheaval and turmoil. Indeed, they assert that the majority of young people (80%) manage the adolescent transition quite well. Nevertheless, these authors also point out that a sizable proportion of adolescents (20%) do not fare so well, with many not receiving the help they may need.

These studies clearly imply that an all-or-none interpretation of adolescence as a period of disturbance is no longer empirically justifiable. We might therefore summarize contemporary research as providing little support for the notion that pathological levels of disturbance predominate during the adolescent years and implying that episodes of emotional upheaval more commonly take place within a framework of developmental normality.

PART TWO:
KEY REASONS FOR STUDYING ADOLESCENCE

A Rationale for Studying Adolescence

A primary reason for studying adolescence is that it is a distinct stage of development during which accelerated, important, and unique changes take place in the biosocial status of the individual (Ansubel, Montmeyor, & Svajian 1977). These writers also suggest that if adolescents as a group tend to feel, learn, think, or act in certain characteristic ways, or if they present common problems of adjustment because they are passing through the same developmental period, then it behooves all persons who have dealings with them to acquire some understanding of the psychology of adolescence. The case for further research also rests upon an estimate by this research team that the ratio of research or theoretical papers published in the field of child development is over twenty-five times more than that for publications on adolescent development. Such a disparity indicates considerable opportunity for expanding research on adolescence before parity of publication is achieved.

Arguments from Review Articles

Although adolescents are often recipients of help, evidence of only limited professional interest in their opinion of helping interventions is long standing. It can be extracted, for example, from Campbell's (1965) review of the counseling literature, which, while discussing twenty-one studies of college students and one of other adults, covered only four investigations involving high school students. Likewise, another early review of research on child psychotherapy done by Barrett, Hampe, and Miller (1978) made no mention of clients' perceptions of their psychotherapy experience and likewise did not specifically address adolescent issues. The later Smith, Glass, and Miller (1980) meta-analysis on the findings of psychotherapy research suggests that this oversight has often been repeated. Out of a total of 420 studies incorporated in this particular analysis, just 32 (i.e., 8% of the total) referred to research carried out with samples of adolescents at the secondary stage of their education, and not one of these studies revealed a significant interest in the opinions of the young people involved.

More recent reviews by Casey and Berman (1985) and Durlak, Fuhrman, and Lampman (1991) have shown concern for the quality of research outcomes for studies carried out within the child population, but have neither incorporated the adolescent age group nor represented consumer opinion. Although Weisz, Weiss, and Donenberg (1992) examined 200 controlled outcome studies which included both younger children and adolescents, as in other reviews, the recipient's perspective did not form the focus of attention. Similarly, a recent review of strategic needs in counseling research (Greenberg 1986) made no mention of adolescent perception. Although McLeod (1990) observed that hardly anyone has asked clients what they think about the help that they have received, this review included only thirteen investigations, none of which incorporated the views of secondary students.

Accordingly, over a period of almost thirty years, reviews of the literature suggest that school-based concerns of students at the secondary level of their education appear to be inadequately represented. Yet adolescent perceptions of personal status represent a useful source of information in helping contexts. They are also of broader theoretical significance. According to Offer, Ostrov, and Howard (1984), research demonstrates that mental health professionals view normal adolescents as markedly more disturbed than the young people involved perceive themselves to be. Nor is the margin of error an insignificant one, since professionals apparently deem normal teenagers to have more problems than either emotionally disturbed or delinquent adolescents actually exhibit. These authors indicate that mental health professionals may erroneously label normal adolescents as being more defensive, more sensitive, more tense, more socially ill at ease, more resentful of criticism, and more easily hurt than young people themselves indicate.

Moreover, while professional judgments have been shown to overestimate the emotionality of adolescents under normal circumstances, equally they underestimate the number of normal adolescents who experienced extremes of emotion. Offer, Ostrov, and Howard (1984) conclude that professional perceptions of normal adolescents resemble the self-descriptions of disturbed teenagers more closely than they do the self-descriptions of normal adolescents. Findings like these suggest there may be a need to ground professional knowledge more securely in studying the perceptions of adolescents themselves.

Arguments from Recent Legal and Policy Developments

In advanced societies, the views of consumers now carry a degree of importance that is previously unparalleled and which needs to be recognized in the delivery of most services, whether individual or corporate, private or public. This thrust now includes education services more than ever before. For example, in the United Kingdom, the 1989 Children Act gives primacy to the views, wishes, and feelings of individual pupils, investing them with legal rights, and enabling them to challenge teacher authority and school practice. It also requires teachers to be more aware of the children in their care, recognizing their individual rights along with their educational needs (Irving & Parker-Jenkins 1995).

With the implementation of the Education Act (1993) which lead to the introduction of the National Curriculum and other central government initiatives, schools have had to accommodate considerable change in the way that they operate. In addition, the Department for Education and Employment (DfEE) Code of Practice, on the identification and assessment of special educational needs, also invokes the need for teachers to take full account of pupils' comments. To comply with the code, schools are required to make every effort to identify the views and wishes of their pupils. The reason given for this ruling is that young people are more likely to respond positively to intervention programs if they fully understand the rationale for their involvement and if they are given some personal responsibility for their own progress (Department for Education and Employment 1994).

Another shift in the way that schools operate is implicit in the policy of the Office for Standards in Education (OFSTED) (1992). This mandates that teams of school inspectors must include the evaluation of pupil support programs in their investigation of every school that they visit. In conducting this evaluation, registered inspectors are specifically directed to sample pupil opinion on the extent to which they benefit from the school's arrangements for guidance and support.

The American school system currently faces concerns over safety that have arisen in the context of multiple shooting incidents, and this has given rise to increased political and professional sensitivity to the needs of children attending school. Indeed, the Educational Excellence for All Act (1999) embraces as one of its key themes the aim of ensuring safe, healthy, disciplined, and drug-free school environments, where all children feel connected, motivated, and challenged to learn. This aim, notes the legislation, requires that school discipline policies focus on prevention, are consistent and fair, and more notably, are developed with the participation of the school community. A legal requirement which charges every school with a clear duty to consult with and otherwise involve its students in addressing these concerns could well be regarded as enlightened, timely, and helpful.

Arguments from Professional Experience

There may, however, be some discrepany between the British government's expectation that schools operate the relevant procedures and professional opinion on the extent to which pupil guidance and support can actually be provided. According to Reid (1989), the U.K. grassroots reality is not only that the demise of school counselors has deprived many schools of a specialist member of staff, but that because the scope and range of children's problems is so great, teachers simply do not have the time to assist every pupil with conduct or emotional problems. Even if they had the time, he argues, the majority of secondary teachers are not properly trained to help, since most training courses offer no course in methods for working with exceptional children, and only a small proportion of teachers have completed relevant in-service courses.

Given these circumstances, it may not be without significance that teachers sometimes report to the author that in the context of responding to National Curriculum priorities, they are unable to spend the time that they would like to on pupil support activities. Yet in the course of his work, the writer has observed that the need for personal support in secondary schools can be predicted for at least some individuals on the basis of their earlier school history. Moreover, interpersonal difficulties may also arise from the transition to secondary education, which is implemented at eleven or twelve years of age by most local education authorities. This imposes a general change in the pattern of pupils' relationships with adults in school, which in itself may carry implications for pupil support. One may note, for example, that during the primary phase of their education, children have to relate consistently to one teacher in one location. This same teacher has responsibility for tasks as diverse as establishing discipline, taking registration, curriculum delivery, and providing personal support. In contrast, within secondary schools, some of these responsibilities are delegated to different members of staff who may be located in widely separated parts of a more complex school campus. From the beginnning of their secondary education, students not unusually find that registration is conducted by one teacher, while curriculum delivery involves as many as a dozen others. Moreover, in the absence of specialized counseling staff, secondary school policies often delegate the tasks of pastoral care, personal and social development, and individual counseling to different teachers again. Serious problems may be rapidly referred to a senior member of the teaching staff. In this situation, secondary students can find that the adult providing help for personal problems is someone whom they do not know well and whose problem-solving role may be compounded by involvement in the school's discipline system.

A Rationale for Studying School-Based Helping

The notion of providing support for individuals having personal difficulties (e.g., with their feelings or relationships) is already well developed in the counseling literature. Notably, Egan (1990) has developed a sophisticated model of practice for counselors which incorporates the notion of helping as its central conceptual pillar. Lazare, Eisenthal, and Wasserman (1975) have suggested that it is the helper's task to enter into a process of negotiation, during which they expect the recipient to state their problem and to give an indication of how they would like to be helped. In outlining an appropriate professional approach, Murgatroyd (1977) suggests that counseling is essentially a helping interaction, in which one person seeks to facilitate the development of self-knowledge and coping strategies in another.

Because of recent legal and operational developments, there is a clear need to take account of the views of young people themselves in planning future provision. The importance of providing appropriate helping resources for children and young persons appears to be recognized by politicians, lawyers, administrators, teachers, counselors, and researchers. On a philosophical note, Bavidge (1995) remarks that although teachers are not social workers, they are very significant in the lives of the children they teach to whom these children look to for normal human care and interest. Although Burningham (1994) suggests that young people will be less able than older people to draw on previous experience, both in terms of understanding their own feelings and in coping with problems that may arise, Branwhite (1988) comments that as long as we do not ask young people for their viewpoint, we stand in danger of implying that their ideas are actually held in low regard.

To achieve general agreement that it is desirable to help young people in need is one thing, but it may be quite another to have sound information upon which to shape the delivery of appropriate resources. As a result of telephone calls placed to the DfEE, the author has learned that pertinent data, for example, on the effectiveness of secondary school counseling services have not been collected systematically. Seemingly, at neither the individual school, local education authority, or national levels of the education service has there been an effort to establish a comprehensive database. In the absence of information on adolescent perceptions of school-based helping, identification of resources and procedures for problem solving with secondary students has until now been largely speculative. Hence the present situation in our schools is in a number of ways unclear. For example, it is hard to know what proportion of adolescents is likely to seek adult help for emotional or interpersonal difficulties in school, what expectations they might hold in seeking help, and what experience and perceptions they have of any help which is on offer. For the reasons discussed, these areas now represent professional issues of considerable importance. Consequently, they are given careful attention in the text that follows. This text presents a wide-ranging review of consumer-focused investigations conducted with secondary school students, and adds challenging new research findings, all of which information is set in a contemporary international context.

2

Research on Adolescent Help Seeking

> On the one hand, seeking the assistance of others has obvious instrumental benefits for the person in need; for example, it is likely to benefit the solution of one's problem. Yet, individuals often refrain from seeking help because of the associated psychological costs. These costs include the public admission of inferiority and dependency.
>
> Nadler 1986a, 976

Insofar as children are guided into asking for help by their parents, we might expect that in the course of growing up, adolescents have become practiced in seeking support from adults. Indeed, we might reasonably expect that they would do so when problems arise in school. Hence, the question arises of how far research may be able to illuminate the overall pattern of adolescent support-seeking behavior.

Lewis (1981) for example suggests an age-related trend in choice of helper during adolescence. In this study, a sample of 108 twelve- to seventeen-year-olds were asked to provide audiotaped advice for a peer. Results indicated that while 21 percent of the 12- to 13-year-olds mentioned referral to an independent specialist, this proportion rose to 46 percent in students who were 15, and to 62 percent by the age of 17. This particular trend was tempered, however, by an interesting parallel. An increasing number of older students also made reference to the possibility that adults have vested interests. The proportion of adolescents supporting this view climbed from 35 percent in the 13- to 14-year-old group, to 48 percent for the 15 year olds, and as high as 74 percent for the 17-year-old students. Although Lewis also reported no age-related change in advice to seek help from parents or peers, this study suggests that it may be prudent to expect conditional adolescent acceptance of adult assistance.

SEEKING SUPPORT FROM TEACHERS

Encouragingly, some studies lend credence to the view that adolescents can at times feel willing to consult with school personnel. From a questionnaire study of 2,046 adolescents in four Manchester comprehensive schools, Murray and Thompson (1985) discovered that 70 percent of the students believed that teachers not only helped them to learn, but also thought that they were willing to listen, to help, and to give good advice. Consonant with the positive aspects of the above study, Raviv et al. (1990) determined that the influence of professionals in schools actually increased during the adolescent years, at least in the domain of formal knowledge.

One notable basis for student consultation with teachers seems likely to be found in the degree of affiliation existing across generations within the classroom. An investigation by Dorhout (1983) concluded that both primary and secondary school pupils valued personal–social characteristics of teachers over their cognitive–intellectual attributes. This study found that it was more important to students that their teachers were friendly or would make the classroom pleasant than that they could think logically or were expert in their subject. Other work by Moos and Trickett (1974) and Fisher and Fraser (1983) underlines an adolescent preference for teacher friendliness rather than teacher authority. High school students in these studies preferred more teacher friendliness but not greater teacher control.

It is significant in this context that two further studies (Galbo 1980; 1983) showed that students drawn from American high school samples were satisfied with the quality of relationship which they experienced with their teachers. In the later of these two investigations, Galbo interviewed a group of thirty-one adolescents (14 males and 17 females) between 16 and 17 years of age, all of whom were able and highly motivated students. In most cases the adolescents in this sample wanted to discuss their problems, ask advice from the significant teacher, or simply share adult company and interests. Whatever the students' goals, however, the adult qualities for which they stated a preference included those of appearing interested, listening, being friendly, showing a sense of humor, and proving trustworthy.

Reinforcement of this pattern of desirable adult qualities emerged from a different research context in a study carried out by Branwhite (1988) which addressed a range of adolescent preferences in secondary school settings. In a sample of 595 adolescents, drawn from six different schools, 58 percent indicated that they had a strong preference for teachers to be empathic in the manner in which they related to students. More specifically, the teacher behaviors that adolescents perceived as demonstrating empathy included being friendly, listening, staying calm, giving encouragement, using humor, and dealing fairly with problems. Three of these features (being friendly, listening, and using humor) are identical with Galbo's (1983) findings despite variations in teenage culture between the United States and the United Kingdom and the substantive difference in the size of the two samples.

Some further appreciation of the position which teachers occupy in the world of adolescents is forthcoming from the work of Bloom and Sosniak (1981). These researchers observed that talented adolescents tended to nominate teachers as among the significant adults in their lives, and likewise, Arnold, Budd, and Miller (1988) noted that 29 percent of their sample of teenagers viewed teachers as an important source of factual career knowledge. Indeed, in reviewing the literature on teachers as significant adults, Galbo (1988) commented that adolescents apparently want teachers to show more interest in them, although this suggestion implies a degree of selectivity on the part of young people attending school. One possible implication is that adolescents only want to become more frequently engaged by the teachers whom they themselves prefer, and Galbo (1994) has reported that adolescents favor caring teachers.

Adolescent preference for teachers who show empathic qualities is also of interest in considering how to develop successful helping approaches with this age group, since empathy is generally regarded as a desirable, if not essential, characteristic for counselors. Hence it might appear that teachers who have adopted empathic behaviors might be sought out by adolescents with personal problems as a major source of support. Yet according to the work of Armacost (1989; 1990), this hypothesis should be viewed with some caution, since it was found that adolescent males perceive classroom teachers as significantly less accessible or sensitive in their interactions with students than did adolescent females. Moreover, available evidence would suggest, perhaps surprisingly, that there is not strong empirical support for the notion that students wish to engage in personally focused consultation with their teachers.

The expectation that adolescents are generally wanting to seek teacher assistance with their personal problems has actually been challenged by some researchers. For example, Galbo (1989) in a review of the literature on adolescent views of teachers as significant others, concluded that not more than 10 percent of adolescents nominate teachers as significant adults in their lives. Moreover, Galbo (1983) found that it was ministers of religion who were the nonrelated adults chosen most frequently by American adolescents as significant others, and Soares and Soares (1974) found significant differences in the way that adolescents perceived themselves and the way they were perceived by their teachers.

Hendry, Roberts, and Glendinning (1992) have suggested that one possible explanation for the reluctance of adolescents to select teachers as significant others may be found in a perception on the part of some students that teachers are more likely to adopt a challenging stance than a supportive one. Continuing this general line of evidence, Berndt and Miller (1989) found that teachers were not among adults regarded as having a significant influence by students in their sample. Likewise, Hendry et al. concluded that Scottish adolescents did not strongly identify teachers as role models for young people in their age group. Furthermore, 50 percent of Murray and Thompson's (1985) sample of Manchester adolescents believed that teachers demonstrated favoritism or bossiness, were boring, and made too many rules. In the most recent study of its type, Keys and Fernandes (1992) reported on the attitudes of just over 2,000 students attending eighty-three U.K. secondary schools, for the National Commission on Education. Among their more significant findings, the authors reported that around 40 percent of the sample had not discussed their own schoolwork (let alone personal problems) with their teachers during the year of the survey.

SEEKING SUPPORT FROM COUNSELORS

It could be hypothesized of course that because of their human relations training, school counselors should enjoy greater student popularity than teachers. Indeed, in support of this proposal, positive early adolescent perspectives on counseling at the secondary level were presented in a small-scale survey completed by Hooper (1978). This study reported on 142 students from a West of England comprehensive school, 50 percent of whom had seen a counselor who followed a client-centered model of practice. Specific reasons given by students for going to see the counselor ranged from difficulty in relationships with teachers (76%); to problems with school work (57%); problems with friends (56%); difficulties with parents (51%); and other unspecified personal issues, (50%). Career items were nominated least frequently (45%) so that interpersonal conflicts appeared to be the major precursor of counselor contact, allowing that the percentages given represent only the consulting students, and not the whole school population.

From a larger scale survey, Armacost (1990) reported that around 80 percent of a 1,301 student sample indicated that teachers were available for help outside of class, although 55 percent stated, in common with secondary students in a number of other surveys, that they would not feel comfortable talking to school staff about personal problems. However, among those individuals in the student body who indicated that they *were* willing to consult secondary-school professionals, 34 percent cited a counselor, 22 percent a sports coach, and 18 percent some other member of the school staff, with only 13 percent nominating a teacher, so that counselors appeared to be the most popular choice by a clear margin.

Modest student support in favor of self-referral to a counselor was reported by Meagher and Clark (1982), who surveyed a sample of 473 secondary students. These workers discovered that while only a minority (12%) emerged as willing to discuss serious personal problems with counselors in school, just a half of this number (6%) reported discussion of personal problems with teachers. A similarly cautious outcome regarding counseling was derived by West et al. (1991) in a survey of 125 Illinois high school students. The largest single group of respondents (29%) indicated that they did not like to tell an unfamiliar individual about personal topics, and 18 percent felt afraid that a school counselor might pass on to other people information which the adolescent conveyed in the course of a personal counseling session. A further 16 percent of the students implied that they would be embarrassed to reveal their real concerns to a school counselor.

Siann, Draper, and Cosford (1982) conducted a Scottish investigation in the form of an analog study, in which only hypothetical problems were considered. Nonetheless, the results indicated an adolescent view that counselors could be effective for resolving school-based concerns, and the authors concluded that adolescents perceived counselors as more likely to be effective in resolving in-school problems. This conclusion was supported by the work of Hutchinson and Reagan (1989). Adolescent perceptions of the positive impact of school counselors also include aspects of school life such as study programs (Haughey & Bowman 1980), class changes, and vocational issues (Murgatroyd 1977; Leviton 1977; Wells & Ritter 1979).

However, further research on adolescent opinion quells any impulse to regard counselors as the major resource for solving the personal problems of adolescents in the school system. For instance,

Remley and Albright (1988), employing interview techniques, trained eleven researchers to gain more in-depth information than could be elicited from questionnaires. In examining the results from forty-four individual student interviews conducted in Virginia, Maryland, and Washington, D.C., they found that students held mainly negative perceptions of high school counselors and were confused as to the counselors' purpose. This untoward finding was backed by Skuy, Hoar, Oakley-Smith, and Westaway (1985), who further concluded from their research that guidance personnel were not regarded by teenage students as being important for any major area of adolescent concern. Leviton (1977) adds to the range of student concerns about being exposed to counseling in school, by attesting to the presence of adolescent anxiety regarding self-disclosure. This survey of 550 Minnesota high school students fifteen to seventeen years old revealed that, whereas just over a half of them would disclose personal problems to a friend, only 4 percent felt willing to do so to a counselor.

The possible existence of an adolescent rationale for selective self-referral to school counselors is buttressed further by an investigation of the attitudes of senior high school students from Indiana, which was completed by Hutchinson and Reagan (1989). These researchers acquired individual ratings from 1,734 respondents in ten randomly selected schools, and the ranking of their accumulated data comes across with considerable impact. From a 24-item rating-scale, the top 10 items were supported from 61 percent to 90 percent of the students, and every one of these items was related to academic and career issues. More intimate concerns such as conflict with peers or the occurrence of personal problems only emerged at or below rank 15 in the data tabulations. This is not to say of course that American high school students in this sample had no personal problems (in fact between 30% and 40% indicated that they did), but the authors found it ironic that while many personal problems were identified, the students obviously felt that they would be more comfortable talking to their counselors about school-related administrative concerns.

The existence of this particular adolescent preference is also upheld by Wells and Ritter (1979), who sought the opinions of 550 adolescent students regarding the appropriateness of certain topics for discussion with a counselor. Once again, academic or administrative issues were classed by about 80 percent of this research sample as suitable discussion topics, while the citation levels for personal or interpersonal problems in contrast remained within single figures. Similarly, Haughey and Bowman (1980) canvassed the views of Canadian students across three separate school districts, only to discover that family problems were not considered as valid for counselor–student review by most of the participants. However, in an outcome which replicated a finding by Leviton (1977), 54 percent of the Canadian sample were ready to discuss truancy with their school counselor, suggesting that perhaps counselors may be valued at times by secondary students because of an inferred capacity to speak for students in the upper reaches of a school's management hierarchy.

It seems possible, however, that there may be something more than personal sensitivity about self-disclosure, or uncertainty regarding counselor trustworthiness, that exercises an important influence on student choice of counselor. While the foregoing studies suggest that specialist counseling services are not likely to be sought by the majority of secondary school students, there is a further source of limitation which needs to be taken into consideration in accounting for adolescent caution regarding professional helpers. As part of the developmental shift away from dependence towards greater independence, there is another group of research studies which demonstrate that the extent of adolescent interaction with adults decreases through the teenage years. This trend has been commented upon by Galbo (1989), who cites supporting evidence from Cervantes (1969); Goodman (1969); Rosenberg (1976); and Newman, Martin, and Petersen (1978). Moreover, it may be added that these sources in turn are chronologically bracketed and reinforced by the investigations of Brittain (1963); Sebald and White (1980); Youniss and Smollar (1985); Wintre et al. (1988); and Hortacsu (1989).

Both adults and adolescents seemingly recognize that the passage through the teenage years can give rise to a variety of problems. Since these problems, however, may only be shared with teachers on a limited basis, the latter set of studies brings to the fore the question of whether adolescents may have alternative human resources open to them for personal support.

SEEKING SUPPORT FROM PEERS

One pragmatic option may be for adolescents to view members of their own peer group as a potential problem-solving resource, and this possibility has received considerable research attention. Adolescent reliance upon the supportive resources of other members of their peer group has been documented by Brittain (1963), Sebald and White (1980), Youniss and Smollar (1985), and Wintre et al. (1988), among others. Raffaelli and Duckett (1989) suggest that the frequency of communication between adolescents increases with age, and Raviv et al. (1990) indicated that it parallels the level attained with parents by the end of the teenage years. This may be a conservative estimate, however, since Csikszentmihalyi and Larson (1984) completed a similar study in which the level of peer communication stood as three times that with family members. The essential point is that these investigations underline the importance which adolescents attribute to communication with their peers.

Other studies suggest that there are clear qualitative as well as quantitative dimensions to peer-level relationships. Brittain (1963) found that peers had a major influence on the type of clothing worn by teenagers and also that they played an influential role in the development of social values. Similarly, Sebald (1986) determined that peers were important in shaping patterns of adolescent social interaction. Striking a note of social relativity, Buhrmester and Furman (1987) concluded from their survey that during adolescence peers become more important as providers of companionship than parents. Sebald (1986) concluded that whereas parents were consulted about money, career, and purchasing issues, peers were the main source of advice regarding social activities and relationships with the opposite sex. In addition, Barnett et al. (1987) noted that adolescents generally favored peers who were empathically motivated over those who helped for nonempathic reasons.

In keeping with this relative point of view, Van Riper (1971) found, from a survey of 735 fourteen year olds, that high school students rated their peers above either classroom teachers or school principals for talking about almost anything, although this argument may need to be tempered by Galbo's (1989) suggestion that adolescents are more likely to communicate with teachers over school-based issues such as academic problems or membership of special interest groups.

Gender preferences may also exercise some influence over choice of helper, even within an adolescent peer group. After canvassing the opinion of 1,972 urban high school students, Robinson et al. (1991) trained eight adolescent students to act as peer counselors. As in a number of studies of adult clients, a higher level of female self-referrals was extant, and overall most students indicated a preference for seeing a female peer counselor. Northman (1985) also found that girls were the most commonly preferred helpers in a mixed-sex sample. However, the intimacy factor did not appear to inhibit communication between adolescent clients and peer counselors to the extent that it often has with adolescents and adult counselors in educational settings, since the range of problems discussed with the former group of helpers included alcohol-related issues, concerns about drugs, worries about parental divorce, and more acutely, questions about suicide.

Nominations of peer support have been found to become more frequent during adolescence (Hortacsu 1989), and the extent of adolescent conformity with peer behavior is thought to peak during midadolescence (Berndt 1979). A general increase in the level of intimacy of relationships with peers has also been reported during the adolescent years, to the point where several studies support the view that by approximately fifteen years of age, adolescent relationships can reflect higher levels of intimacy than those that prevail between teenage children and their parents (see, for example, La Gaipa 1979; Kon & Losenkov 1978; Reisman & Shorr 1978; and Hunter and Youniss 1982).

SEEKING SUPPORT FROM FRIENDS

In terms of the quality of relationships between adolescents and their peers, friendship links should also have an important part to play, since their very existence suggests that an intimacy dynamic could influence the quality of communication taking place between young people. In this connection, it has been reported that during the adolescent years, friends are preferred to parents as a source of company during leisure time (Wright & Keple 1981). Indeed, the same authors found that girls reported how they also regarded their friends as more rewarding to be with than their parents. Similarly, in the investigation of Millen and Roll (1977), boys have indicated that they view their male friends as having equal or superior standing to their mothers, and same-sex friends have been identified, along with mothers, as preferred targets for communication (Hortacsu 1989).

Kandel and Lesser (1969b) have also recorded an adolescent preference for friends as a source of advice for personal problems, while Friedman (1991) noted that friends were identified as the most important source of advice for over one-third of the fifteen- to seventeen-year-old adolescents in his sample. Gordon and Grant's (1997) Glasgow survey showed that friends were referred to three to four times more often than parents in talking over negative feelings. It has also been suggested that for the purpose of seeking advice regarding relationships with their peers, adolescents regard their friends as generally having more to offer than their parents (Hunter 1985). The work of Blyth, Hill, and Thiel (1982) has implied that adolescents favor relationships with friends of both the same age and the same sex as a source of personal support, a proposition upheld by Rivenbark (1971) who detected higher levels of intimacy prevailing within same-sex relationships during adolescence. Thus it appears that young people widely regard their friends as an important means of assistance, with the possible exception of cross-sex relationships during late adolescence, a situation for which an increase in problems has been reported (Stark et al. 1989).

SEEKING SUPPORT FROM PARENTS

Insofar as patterns of communication are initially acquired at home and have to be maintained over time in order that personal needs can be met as children grow older, it seems reasonable to expect that adolescents might build on past experience to seek advice from other family members. A number of studies bear this expectation out. Parents have been nominated as an important source of support by adolescents in the research samples of Wintre et al. (1988); Friedman (1991); and Hendry, Roberts, and Glendinning (1992); while Sebald (1986) noted in a longitudinal study that although there had been a downturn in adolescent orientation to parents during the 1960s and 1970s, a recovery took place during the 1980s. Indeed, there is evidence that both sexes regard their parents as the primary source of practical wisdom available to them (Kandel & Lesser 1969a; Kon & Losenkov 1978), including when making decisions about their future life (Smith 1976).

Although this assumption may appear to be supported mainly by the work of American researchers (see for instance Berndt & Miller 1989), in fact it is bolstered further by some recent U.K. studies. Studies by Porteous and Fisher (1980) and Siann, Draper, and Cosford (1982) have found that British adolescents mention parents frequently as available sources of help. This finding had been repeated in a survey of 360 eleven to sixteen year olds carried out a over a decade later by Hendry, Roberts, and Glendinning (1992), and in a sample of 1,634 adolescents of 13.5 to 14.5 years by Gordon and Grant (1997). Whitney and Smith (1992) have reported that secondary level students are significantly more likely to tell someone at home that they have been bullied than they are to tell a teacher. Similarly, Keys and Fernandes (1993) noted that in a national sample of 2,140 secondary students from years seven and nine, over two-and-one-half times as many adolescents indicated that they had consulted parents for career advice as had approached teachers on the same topic.

SEEKING SUPPORT FROM MOTHERS

Research suggests that as far as parent contact goes, there is a tendency for adolescents to favor consulting their mothers. Hendry, Roberts, and Glendinning (1992) reported that mothers have been identified by 56 percent of their sample of teenage children as their most significant family member. Kandel and Lesser (1969b) have identified a high level of influence and close concordance of values between adolescents and their mothers. There are indications that young people are more open with their mothers (Barnes & Olsen 1985) and disclose more to them (Wiebe and Williams 1972; Youniss & Ketterlinus 1987). For advice on complex problems, mothers have been nominated as the resource person of first choice by both sexes (Kon & Losenkov 1978; Kandel & Lesser 1969b). However, in contrast to boys, girls have reported doing more decision making with their mothers and having a more satisfactory relationship with them (Newman 1989). Likewise, in Gordon and Grant's (1997) study, recourse to maternal advice was reportedly sought by over twice as many female compared to male students.

Adolescents perceive their mothers' expertise to encompass social relationships, general knowledge about life, personal feelings, and conventions about appearance, (Raviv et al. 1990) while they also experience them as more accepting and more understanding in handling problems (Youniss & Smollar 1985). Given this information, it is hardly surprising that other investigators have found that during their teenage years children communicate more frequently with their mothers (Barnes & Olsen 1985) and report in turn a higher level of satisfaction with the communication they receive from maternal sources.

SEEKING SUPPORT FROM FATHERS

As might be anticipated from the previous paragraph, contemporary research suggests that adolescents appear somewhat less appreciative of their fathers in relation to solving personal problems. Nonetheless, areas of expertise attributed by young persons to their fathers include formal knowledge, science, and politics (Raviv et al. 1990) and they are a recognized source of practical advice, even if not employed for this purpose to quite the extent that mothers have been (Kandel & Lesser 1969b; Kon & Losenkov 1978). Moreover, Wright and Keple (1981) found that adolescents perceived their fathers to be no less responsive or helpful when approached than were their mothers; fathers, however, have been identified by teenage sons and daughters as inclined to initiate fewer conversations than mothers, to give less recognition to issues of adolescent concern (Noller & Callan 1990), and also to communicate in a more judgmental manner (Youniss & Smoller 1985).

Adolescent girls have indicated that their fathers did not provide as much personal support as their mothers (Wright & Keple 1981) and that their fathers did not seem to know them as individuals as well as their mothers did (Youniss & Ketterlinus 1987). Fathers seem to gain somewhat greater credit from boys, who have been found by Hunter and Youniss (1982) to be more nurturing than mothers. Nevertheless, boys report disclosing equivalent amounts of personal information to both male and female parents (Wiebe & Williams 1972).

Somewhat paradoxically, boys have also reported (Wright & Keple 1981) that their father is more difficult to get along with than their mother, suggesting that sex differences in adolescent opinion are not clear cut, at least to the extent that either same-sex or oppo-site-sex support are universally preferred. Indeed, even the prefer-ence for parental assistance is not a universal one, since parents are not favored as helpers by every student in the studies referred to. Northman's (1985) survey of 238 New York eight to nineteen year olds in fact found that a generally low rating of parents as effective helpers was unaffected by student age, sex, or problem situation. Furthermore, this somewhat adverse trend in research findings also needs to be understood in the context of a review by Phares and Compas (1992), which implicates both mothers and fa-thers, but notably the latter, in the development of adolescent psy-chopathology.

SYNOPSIS OF RESEARCH ON SEEKING SUPPORT IN ADOLESCENCE

The available literature suggests that when adolescents have problems, they are likely to seek support both within and between generations of potential helpers. However, this process often ap-pears to be conducted on a selective basis. Regardless of the expec-tations that as concerned professionals we might hold regarding our ability to support young people, available evidence nonetheless suggests that adolescents do not regard us as the helpers of first choice.

STUDIES FEATURING SUPPORT FROM PEERS

A breakdown of the research in this area reveals that for per-sonal problems, adolescents most frequently seek support from oth-ers in their own age group. Almost twenty years of adolescent consumer studies supporting this contention include those of Barnett et al. (1987); Berndt (1979); Blyth, Hill, and Theil (1982); Bo (1989); Buhrmester and Furman (1987); Csikszentmihalyi and Larson (1984); Frankel (1990); Gordon and Grant (1997); Hendry,

Roberts, and Glendinning (1992); Herriott (1963); Rivenbark (1971); Sebald (1986); Van Riper (1971); and Wright and Keple (1981).

STUDIES FEATURING SUPPORT FROM PARENTS

Further studies were found in which parents constituted the favored group of resource persons for adolescents with personal problems, and these likewise incorporated research reported over two decades, including that of Barnes and Olsen (1985); Eme, Maisiak, and Goodale (1979); Gordon and Grant (1997); Hendry, Roberts, and Glendinning (1992); Hunter and Youniss (1992); Noller and Bagi, (1985); Noller and Callan (1990); Porteous and Fisher (1980); Siann, Draper, and Cosford (1982); Simpson (1962); Wiebe and Williams (1972); Youniss and Ketterlinus (1987); and Youniss and Smollar (1985).

STUDIES FEATURING SUPPORT FROM
PARENTS AND FRIENDS

A third set of research investigations attests to an adolescent tendency to discuss personal difficulties both with parents and with friends. This set includes three decades of research completed by Arnold, Budd, and Miller (1988); Brittain (1963); Friedman (1991); Gordon and Grant (1997); Hendry, Roberts, and Glendinning (1992); Hortacsu (1989); Hunter (1985); Kandel and Lesser (1969b); Keats et al. (1983); Kon and Losenkov (1978); Murgatroyd (1977); Raffaelli and Duckett (1989); Raja, McGee, and Stanton (1991); Raviv et al. (1990); Wilks (1986); and Wintre et al. (1988). It therefore appears that different categories of helpers need not be used on a mutually exclusive basis and that informal sources of support are widely employed for helping with personal problems.

STUDIES FEATURING SUPPORT FROM
SCHOOL PROFESSIONALS

Studies in which adolescents with personal problems favor discussion with school personnel do not seem to be an outstanding feature of this body of research literature. Hence it is tempting to conclude that in the domain of personal problems, the influence of teachers is often outweighed by the influence of parents and peers. Indeed, this indication of a trend away from professional helpers is sustained by two separate lines of inquiry. First, it is upheld by investigations indicating that adolescents with personal problems did not want to discuss them with teachers (Galbo 1980, 1983;

Hendry, Roberts, & Glendinning 1992; Laframboise, Dauphinais, & Rowe 1978). Second, it is reinforced by further studies revealing that adolescents avoided initiating counselor contact (Hutchinson & Reagan 1989; Leviton 1977; Meagher & Clark 1982; Wells & Ritter 1979; West et al. 1991).

Before dismissing the supportive role of professional helpers completely, however, it is important to note adolescent opinion supporting their involvement for educational and career issues. Six studies have portrayed student willingness to seek related advice from teachers (Arnold, Budd, & Miller 1988; Galbo 1980, 1983; Laframboise, Dauphinais, & Rowe 1978; Murgatroyd 1977; Raviv et al. 1990). An additional four studies reveal readiness to consult school counselors for the same reasons (Haughey & Bowman 1980; Hutchinson & Reagan 1989; Leviton 1977; Wells & Ritter 1979). Two more investigations suggest that specialist careers personnel are valued for their professional advice (Arnold, Budd, & Miller 1988; Cherry & Gear 1987).

In addition, parents have been identified by adolescents as helpful regarding educational and career matters by eight investigations (Cherry & Gear 1987; Friedman 1991; Hendry, Roberts, and Glendinning 1989; Hunter 1988; Raviv et al. 1990; Sebald 1986; Smith 1976; Wilks 1986). One or two more studies found that friends were considered as an additional source of assistance in deciding upon academic issues (Friedman 1991; Van Riper 1971). Once again, these studies suggest some variety in adolescent choice of helper.

CONCLUSION

There could be several possible explanations as to why young people of school age are selective in choosing others as sources of support. To begin with, their peers (notably those counted as friends) can offer a high proportion of shared experience. Peers can also be involved in adolescent experience with a degree of recency that adults cannot. Support seeking is also likely to be influenced by the availability of helping agents. For example, mothers may offer a window of opportunity which is much greater than school professionals are able to provide (notably, in that, while schools are open only for a limited number of days a year, parents are likely to be available every day).

Quality of relationship (e.g., in terms of intimacy) is also likely to be influential, since this enables teenagers to judge the extent to which they can trust any potential helper to understand and support them. Clearly, professionals, friends, and relatives provide differing levels of intimacy, formality, and responsiveness. Professionals may also be handicapped in the world of adolescence because of multiple demands upon their time, which means that they may not be able to provide longer-term support in the way that parents or friends often can. Overall, it seems likely that a number of factors may render education professionals less attractive as sources of support for adolescents with personal problems.

This is not of course to say that secondary students never seek help from school-based helpers. The author has in fact observed such requests being made of teachers and had many more reported by senior teaching staff. Indeed, the issues dealt with can reflect an acute state of student need. It therefore appears possible that the availability of significant others may operate as a filter system which is robust enough to contain the majority of low-level student problems and hassles. However, where interpersonal attachments are poorly developed or are not available at the time of need and when problems are sufficiently acute, recourse to formal support options may be rendered relatively more attractive and more probable.

3

Research on Adolescent Perception

One way to acquire insight into the nature of contemporary youth and their problems would be to focus on the quality of the relationship between youth and adults. Since this relationship has been viewed as absolutely essential to the development of youth, valuable information could be obtained through understanding youths' attitudes toward the adults they perceive as important.

Galbo 1983, 417–418

Mann and Borduin (1991) in a critique of psychotherapy research on adolescent clients have argued that future investigations with adolescents should pay increased attention to client-related factors, since these may moderate treatment outcomes to a significant extent. Accordingly, emphasis will next be given to those studies that have reported adolescent perceptions of the help they have received. The majority of the investigations (in this case approximately two-thirds of them) have been carried out during the last ten years, suggesting considerably increased interest in adolescent opinion in this decade, as opposed to the previous.

PATTERNS OF SERVICE USAGE

Chapter 2 included numerous findings suggesting that adolescents can be selective in seeking support from professional helpers.

Here we will consider another group of studies which indicates that secondary students may at times approach school professionals for support regarding their personal problems. For example, Hooper (1978) reported that in a survey of 142 students in an English secondary school, problems with teachers formed the most common reason for student referral to a school counselor. Accordingly, research on student perceptions of the help they have received forms the substance of the next area to be considered.

A large-scale investigation has been reported by Gray (1980). This author provides data on a sample of 3,870 Scottish school leavers for the academic year 1971–1972, together with a further sample of 7,992 Highland leavers for 1975–1976. From the earlier sample, between 56 and 58 percent of the students felt that their teachers had known them well enough to provide advice on educational or career matters. In comparison, only 19 percent of that sample nominated teachers as advisors for personal problems. (Hence three times more students indicated acceptance of teacher advice on technical matters than on personal issues.)

A similar outcome was derived from the 1975–1976 adolescent sample, in that the majority (up to 57% of the students) indicated that they had received help from teachers and guidance personnel on educational and career issues, while only a small proportion (10%) reported that they had received teacher assistance with personal problems. (In this case, almost six times more students received technical advice from teachers than accepted personal support.) Moreover, even with educational and career problems, a higher proportion of students (65% to 76%) cited parents as a source of help, while 43 percent mentioned receiving the assistance of siblings and friends, as well as that of other relatives. Gray concluded from his data that there seemed to be considerable uncertainty on the part of both the Scottish teachers and their pupils about the extent to which the school as an institution should be involved in the personal concerns of students.

In relation to contact with school counselors, rather than teachers, Lehmanowsky (1991) presented the results of a 33 percent random sample (N = 507) of the 1,521 students attending a high school in Lincoln, Nebraska. This survey followed the implementation of a new service delivery model that included a shift in emphasis away from students always seeing a specific counselor toward a more open topic-specialist service. At the end of the school year during which this change was introduced, 82 percent of the sample indicated that they had received assistance from the counseling service, and 90 percent of these students reported liking the option of working with a counselor of their own choice.

From a later survey (M. B. Lehmanowsky 1992, personal communication) the same researcher was able to report findings from a different sample of students (N = 984) in the same high school. In this case, 55 percent of the students sought counseling regarding academic issues. By comparison, only 19 percent had made contact regarding personal problems, yielding a 3:1 ratio, favoring technical over personal support. These findings compare closely with the results obtained by Gray (1980) for educational isues and also for personal issues in the first of the two Scottish samples reported. The level for assistance with personal problems in Gray's second sample was much lower.

Further variation in adolescent opinion is shown by Hutchinson and Reagan (1989). In an analysis of the use of school counselors among 1,734 Indiana senior high school students, around 40 percent reported that they would go to a counselor about general personal problems. In some contrast, Meagher and Clark's (1982) survey of 473 students attending an Ohio high school revealed that only 6 percent of their sample recorded that they had discussed a serious personal problem with a counselor. Moreover, Abal and Hornby (1995) reported that in a sample of 300 secondary students in Kuwait, while 70 percent suggested that educational issues were important for counselors, over a third did not consider that counseling for personal problems was important.

Hannon et al. (1983) (also cited in O'Leary 1990) similarly confirmed that counselors were the main source of help over career choices for 95 percent of the final year Irish secondary students whom they surveyed. Once again, however, it is important to take account of evidence that other sources of help are likely be called upon by secondary school students. Sproles (1988), reporting on a survey of 200 West Virginia high school students, found that while 24 percent of her sample indicated that counselors had been helpful with career choices, parent support was alluded to by 49 percent, and teacher support by 62 percent, while 72 percent referred to assisting themselves. This study suggests that secondary students may use multiple sources of information in making career decisions.

These studies, though few in number, tend to support the proposition that the majority of adolescents do not discuss personal problems with either teachers or school counselors, at least according to data from Scotland, Ireland, and the United States. Paradoxically, this outcome is probably a helpful one from the point of view of many school professionals involved in student support, for whom the demand to provide quality support for the whole of a school population might prove difficult to meet. Having fewer student referrals to contend with could mean that a higher quality of service may be provided for those whose need is greatest.

STUDENT TAKE-UP RATES

Even if it were a desirable objective, the task of wholesale engagement of adolescent clients is unlikely to be an easy one, since the evidence on take-up rates for professional support suggests considerable variation. Studies providing percentage data on adolescent take-up rates, without specifying the type of problem involved, have identified from 14 percent (Morey et al. 1989), to 50 percent (Hooper 1978; Sproles 1988) to 82 percent (Lehmanowsky 1991) as having received some form of counseling input. Newport (1977) concluded that in schools with a counseling service, an overall 42 percent of the students indicated that they had used it. However, it was also found that 29 percent reported using community support systems, such as those for youth or social services. Porteous and Fisher (1980) published related data broken down by profession for their small-scale Bradford sample. This showed that 23 percent had approached teachers about a problem, 5 percent a social worker, 3 percent a youth worker, 3 percent a family doctor, and 3 percent a religious worker.

Seven further investigations refer specifically to educational and career issues. Sample proportions reporting the receipt of professional support ranged from 15 percent, 24 percent, and 25 percent (Newport 1977; Sproles 1988; Hutchinson & Bottorff 1986); to 40 percent, 55 percent, and 58 percent (M. B. Lehmanowsky 1992, personal communication; Gray 1980); and as high as 95 percent (Hannon et al. 1983; Murray & Thompson 1985).

Another group of six surveys report personal reasons for seeking support. These yield much lower figures of 6 percent (Meagher & Clark 1982) and 10 percent (Gray 1980); to 15 percent (Newport 1977), 19 percent, and 21 percent (Gray 1980; M. B. Lehmanowsksy 1992, personal communication; Hutchinson & Bottorff 1986); and up to 50 percent (Seifert 1985). These studies support earlier research suggesting that adolescents disclose more regarding school-based concerns (West 1975; White 1974).

Student take-up rates clearly vary considerably between studies. However, by averaging out the data from the above studies, it appears that approximately 51 percent of the students met a counselor to sort out educational or career issues, whereas only 20 percent saw a counselor to deal with personal concerns. In contrast with these figures, Neely and Iburg (1989) reported that 60 percent of their adolescent referrals were for personal reasons, an estimate which runs counter to the trend across the other studies. Their sample size was small, however (N = 20 students), and their figures were based upon data derived from counselors rather than directly from the students themselves.

It therefore appears that approximately four-fifths of the secondary students responding to published surveys have elected not to discuss personal problems with teachers or counselors in school. However, the remaining one-fifth is a proportion which is probably no less important than the equivalent proportion of U.K. students having special educational needs. Moreover, there appears to be no prima facie reason why students' personal needs should be regarded as any less deserving of support in school, despite the fact that a different cohort of students may be involved.

LEVEL OF NEED AND SERVICE PROVIDED

Given that empathic interaction is one of the ideals of the counseling movement, it might be anticipated that few exceptions to this quality of personal assistance would be reported. However, Hutchinson and Bottorff (1986) suggest that significant numbers of students may not have received the level of service which they believed themselves to require. This research team developed a questionnaire about high school counseling services (on the basis of three 2-hour discussions with a pool of 70 university students) which was administered to a further 250 Indiana undergraduates, who were drawn from 21 states, and represented a client sample from 152 high school counseling programs.

Indicated differences between the numbers of students who actually received a service in high school against those who needed it turned out to be considerable. As many as 89 percent of this Indiana sample indicated that they needed career counseling but only 40 percent reported that they had received it. Although 60 percent stated that they had needed personal counseling during the high school phase of their education, just 21 percent said that this service had been forthcoming.

On the other hand, it did not seem uncommon for students to be assigned a service which they did not require. Counselors were reported as having delivered some form of educational testing to 37 percent of the sample when a mere 10 percent had wanted it. A record-keeping emphasis was referred to in 24 percent of the cases, but only 3 percent had listed this as a personal requirement. Finally, 20 percent had been the subject of attendance checks where merely 1 percent felt that this was warranted. Thus, as far as direct counseling services were concerned, there was a discrepancy between student requirement and counselor service delivered in-between 39 percent and 49 percent of the instances recorded. With indirect counseling services, the range of discrepancy spanned 19 to 27 percent of the examples reported. It might be inferred from the data that student concerns were either not identified by the school counseling staff involved or that they were not a major priority on the professional agenda of the counselors involved.

EVALUATION OF HELP RECEIVED

A small number of studies have set out to explore adolescent views of helping experiences, and clearly secondary students do not lack ideas about the efficacy of the counseling input to which they have been exposed. For example, Poppen and Peters (1965) found that junior high school students expected to receive more advice than they were given when they talked to school counselors, whereas counselors placed more emphasis upon establishing working relationships.

An important determinant of opinion among secondary students may be whether or not counselors deliver the services for which they carry responsibility. Wiggins and Moody (1987) carried out a large-scale survey of the population of seven suburban and four rural high schools distributed across four American states, randomly selecting 20 to 25 percent of the students at each school for a one-hour interview. Several interesting findings emerged. First, in schools receiving the highest student approval ratings, counselors spent just over 70 percent of their professional time in counseling activities, reporting that only 11 to 12 percent were assigned to administrative functions. Second, those counselors who spent most of their time in direct contact with students were rated as more effective. This finding suggests that there may be an interaction between counselor commitment, counselor competencies, and positive student perceptions.

Third, the schools rated as average or above average by their student population were those in which counselors worked through referred problems promptly. In practice this meant within a range of one to five sessions each of twenty to thirty minutes in duration so that a total of two-and-one-half hours of counseling time was the maximum student commitment involved. Although student ratings varied to some extent across schools, these findings remained unaffected by differences in the counselor–client ratio between research locations. Fourth, the proportion of students indicating that they would recommend counselor assistance to a good friend varied according to the type of problem under consideration. Over 70 percent stated that they would make such a recommendation for either an academic or a career concern, compared to 27 percent for a personal concern.

Another factor to take into account may be found in the interaction between personal motivation of the student and their assessment of counseling. Seifert (1985) surveyed 1,244 students from secondary, lower commercial, and vocational schools in Austria and concluded that there was a significant relationship between their readiness to participate and their perception of the quality of the program received. While students with a higher level of vocational maturity appeared to derive more benefit from the guidance program, from the consumer perspective a more interesting finding was that over 50 percent of the sample indicated a need for more intensive personal counseling.

Nonetheless, evidence remains to suggest that there is widespread reservation on the part of adolescent consumers regarding the efficacy of counseling interventions. One substantial study which speaks to this issue is that of Chase (1981), who conducted a large-scale survey of 10,478 high school students in twenty-two states of the United States. Although the majority of the respondents were satisfied with their treatment by counselors, 33 percent indicated that they were unhappy with school counseling services. One reason given to explain the sense of dissatisfaction was a lack of help from counselors in solving personal problems. Students also remarked how they felt that neither school administrators, teachers, nor counselors took a sufficiently strong interest in them as individuals.

ADOLESCENT SATISFACTION

An early investigation by Newport (1977) was carried out on 148 sixth-form students in five New Zealand secondary schools. In this investigation, a range of academic, career, and personal issues had been the focus of requests for counselor assistance on the part of the students. However, in one of the few interview studies to be reported, this researcher found that only 24 percent of her sample believed their needs were met by school professionals. The later investigation of Gray (1980) also reported a low level of adolescent satisfaction, with just under a fifth of the sample indicating that personal advice received from guidance teachers had been useful. In a different context, Wells et al. (1978) found that 65 percent of forty teenagers attending an adolescent unit felt that they had sorted their problems out. In this study, however, the follow-up periods varied from six to twenty-six months after discharge, so the opinions gathered were not contiguous with the intervention provided.

In a study of peer counseling, Morey et al. (1989) sampled the opinions of 126 students from a high school in the Rocky Mountains. Around 50 percent of these adolescents had presented a specific problem during their initial session, mostly to do with educational concerns (65%), although there was also a high rate of referral concerning cross-sex relationships (52%). The least frequently raised topics included alchohol or drug-related issues (22% and 21% respectively). Three-quarters of the sample also reported that they were not embarrassed in talking to a peer counselor, and 57 percent indicated that peer counselors were good listeners. However, only 38 percent believed that peer counselors had in turn been worth listening to. Mean ratings of satisfaction with counselor helpfulness were highest regarding educational or career issues and lowest in connection with drug or alcohol problems. The authors concluded that training in listening skills was a necessary but not a sufficient condition for helping students to deal with the concerns of their peers.

Probably the most extensive survey of adolescent satisfaction to date has been executed by Engen, Laing, and Sawyer (1988) who analyzed the opinions of 31,419 high school students. Their 10 percent random sample, distributed across eastern, central, and western areas of the United States, covered ten consecutive years between 1973 and 1984. This research team was able to report that they discovered a steady increase in student satisfaction with guidance counseling, rising from 48 percent in 1973–1974 to 59 percent in 1983–1984. Moreover, no significant relationships emerged between the level of student satisfaction and other variables. These included the type of high school involved, the kind of instructional program received (vocational or college orientated), the student's ethnic group, the student's academic rankings in high school, the student's perceived adequacy of their educational program in high school, their need for career planning assistance, or their need for help to handle personal concerns. The researchers went on to perform a multiple regression analysis on a subsample of 588 students to determine whether it would be possible to predict student satisfaction with guidance counseling, but no statistically significant relationships could be detected. Sex, race, class rank, and other variables were apparently unrelated to student satisfaction levels.

It almost goes without saying that since these investigations derive from different circumstances and are not of the same scope, comparison of their findings would be an exercise of dubious validity. Moreover, the main body of the research has been carried out in the United States, providing a limited basis for generalization of the findings across other cultures.

ADOLESCENT AND PROFESSIONAL VIEWS

A very small number of researchers have conducted counseling investigations which have compared opinions of adolescents with those of adults. De Weerdt (1986), for example, surveyed 45 teachers and 173 students in two Dutch secondary schools. The education system in Holland mandates that all counselors are also classroom teachers, and the reported professional ethos is that teachers assume a high level of professional responsibility for the personal development of students. In this European context, both students and teachers agreed that counseling was an appropriate resource for addressing personal problems, and there was a high level of agreement among students regarding the goals of counseling. Over 75 percent of the student sample indicated that counseling meant immediate support, careful attention, reliability, vocational guidance, and the availability of advice or information.

There were also some interesting differences between the views of adolescents and adults in this study. For example, students expressed more satisfaction with the services received than teachers were aware of. In addition, students perceived more results to accrue from counseling than did teachers, while fewer students than teachers thought that changes in the dropout rate or improvements in client–counselor relationship would result from counseling. In some ways the adolescent worldview also seemed more pragmatic, in that a smaller proportion of students was identified as expecting dedicated commitment from their teachers than was apparent among the teachers themselves.

Another publication comparing the views of adolescents with those of adults has resulted from the work of Taylor, Adelman, and Kayser-Boyd (1986), who investigated twenty-four client–therapist dyads drawn from a special school population of students with learning, emotional, and behavioral difficulties. As is the case with many special school populations, there was a predominance of male students in this sample, which contained twenty male and four female students whose ages ranged from eleven to nineteen years. From the participant's responses to a twenty-eight-item rating scale, the researchers were able to draw several enlightening conclusions. Having observed that there was agreement between both the therapists and the clients that the establishment of conditions for trust was a particularly important feature of the counseling set up, the research team noted that the client group also agreed with the therapists regarding the importance of warmth, a client-driven agenda, and the importance of an emphasis upon client needs.

Against the therapist-group ratings, these students tended to go to the more extreme points of the rating scale. However, it also transpired that student ratings on the subscales relevant to counseling climate demonstrated a modest positive correlation with the amount of time spent on critical issues during the initial stage of counselor contact. In general, adolescent clients who experienced the help given as enhancing their autonomy gave significantly higher ratings on satisfaction at the end of the program, and likewise, those who perceived therapy as warm and enhancing personal responsibility also rated therapy as more important.

Hagborg and Konigsberg (1991) carried out another comparative investigation of adolescent opinion within a special education setting. In this case the subjects were forty-five students enrolled in a school for emotionally disturbed adolescents in New York. The students completed a ten-item rating scale, which yielded several significant outcomes. Students' perceptions of counseling, after a minimum of twenty individual sessions, were comparable with those of teachers, in that both groups associated progress with school attendance. Students viewed therapeutic progress to be greater, however, than did teachers, and they did not relate changes occurring in the course of therapy to their academic status, to the presence of conduct disorder, or to high levels of psychological distress, as did both teachers and therapists.

An additional study carried out within a population of emotionally disturbed and learning-disabled young adolescents (Kayser-Boyd, Adelman, & Taylor 1985) concluded that these students were able to identify both the risks and benefits of professional counseling. Identified risks were linked with self-disclosure (23%); discomfort with the professional helper (15%); violation of confidence (13%); and a perception of low therapeutic effectiveness (10%). Offsetting these views, commonly identified benefits included opportunities to solve problems (39%); having someone to talk to (27%); and learning new things (13%). These findings probably go some way toward explaining why forty out of the sixty-two students sampled also indicated some willingness to take part in further counseling.

Changing any negative perceptions of professional support in this segment of the school population may not be an easy undertaking, however, according to an interview study of thirty-two young adolescents in special education settings, which was carried out by the same research team (Taylor, Adelman, & Kayser-Boyd 1985). From this investigation, the researchers noted that reluctance and dissatisfaction were encountered at various stages of the helping interview among 79 percent of their sample. These students gave various reasons for holding an adverse opinion. Some of these reasons related to aspects of the counseling process, such as being asked too many questions, feeling pressured, or causing more problems. Other reasons given by the students related to aspects of themselves, such as having no personal problems or feeling no need of professional help. Further justification referred to the way in which the counseling process was presented, such as having little choice about turning up, being coerced into attending, or being faced with sanctions for not showing up. These features may be more commonly encountered in school-based referrals because, in the author's experience, they sometimes carry disciplinary overtones.

In parallel with the work carried out by other researchers in this area, Friedman, Glickman, and Kovach (1986) surveyed another adolescent group from a special population. These workers drew upon the experiences of 482 sixteen-year-old participants in thirty outpatient and twenty-seven residential drug-treatment programs, comparing their views with those of the project staff involved. Generally speaking, female adolescents rated the treatment programs which they had participated in more positively than did their male counterparts. A more intriguing outcome in light of expected differences between adult and adolescent perceptions, however, was that both clients and staff rated residential programs more highly, apparently because of a perception of extra personal support, increased levels of concern, and greater encouragement of the client's expression of negative feelings.

In working with underachieving students, Mills (1985) found that they identified hobbies as the best topic to talk about, followed by relationships with others, while the worst topic of conversation involved discussion of unhappy times students had experienced. Noting that underachievers have more difficulty with expressing themselves, Mills also observed that her students disclosed more information where self-disclosure had been modeled.

ADOLESCENT TERMINATION OF CONTACT

Two investigations outside of the school setting have suggested that technical attributes of the session set up can influence the way in which professional helping is perceived by adolescent consumers. For example, the majority of English adolescents interviewed by Stuart-Smith (1994), while indicating that they had benefited from support in an adolescent unit, objected to the use that had been made of a one-way mirror and video equipment. A similar finding from the Texas study of Newfield et al. (1991) was that their teenage clients particularly disliked the use of video cameras to record the sessions. This sample of young people reported feeling scared during initial sessions, and the researchers observed that a common adolescent tactic was to listen carefully in the early phase of professional contact and to gather information on their parent's position which was later actively employed between sessions in attempts to obstruct further family participation. These Texan adolescents unanimously reported themselves as being against therapy carried out in a family context.

A study of the premature termination of contact in an Irish high school context (O'Leary 1979) reminds us that adolescents should not be thought of as a homogenous group. O'Leary tracked and interviewed 123 fifteen- to nineteen-year-old students over a one-year period, which is a much longer period of association between investigator and client group than is found in most studies. Although from a student perspective helper empathy emerged as an important consideration, another critical outcome was that 45 percent of the students chose to terminate contact with their counselor as early as the second counseling session. Consequently, it would seem that that some variability of response may be expected among adolescent consumers. O'Leary also compared terminating students with those who continued in counseling and concluded that terminators were those who had negative attitudes toward people in general as well as toward counseling and were unable to accept help from either formal or informal sources. This analysis, however, provided no data on patterns of informal helping, and it left unanswered the question of what types of adolescent reasoning produced an early termination decision.

Suzuki (1989) examined records at the Tavistock Clinic in London to determine rates of premature termination in a sample of 105 clients of between fourteen and twenty-two years of age. Approximately 25 percent dropped out at the assessment–interview stage, and 20 percent made a unilateral decision to terminate contact. Almost half the sample (49%) dropped out of treatment prior to session twelve of their counseling program. From these data, Suzuki drew a parallel with dropout rates in adult clients, who have been reported by Garfield (1978) as engaging in a median number of between five and six counseling sessions.

Perhaps feedback on the extent to which students terminate counseling prematurely may offer an indirect index of their satisfaction with the counseling process, and a small number of investigations bear upon this issue. For instance, Vial-Val et al. (1984) reported that 73 percent of 102 fifteen-year-olds terminated unilaterally before session seventeen, and as many as 65 percent of the students surveyed by Morey et al. (1989) dropped out after either one or two sessions, like 45 percent of the students in O'Leary's (1979) study. Accordingly, the question of how to attract students to helping services and maintain their commitment appears to be an issue of no small importance.

ADOLESCENT AVOIDANCE OF HELP

Although there are a number of reports of positive adolescent perceptions of adult assistance, it is clear that numerous individuals terminate contact prematurely, and many other teenagers do not seek formal help to begin with. In Suzuki's (1989) study, for instance, 17 percent of the adolescent clients failed to show up for even their first appointment. Attention must therefore be given to hypotheses that seek to explain their avoidance of helping interventions.

In addressing factors that may prevent or disturb contact with professional helpers, West et al. (1991) indicate that adolescent preparation and orientation may be important. From a survey of 235 students attending Illinois high schools, these writers suggested that students who are unprepared for adult support or who have negative attitudes toward it may be unaware of the objectives and benefits involved. Potential clients, they point out, are unlikely to seek help unless these deficits and apprehensions are resolved. It was also noted that the strongest student responses reflected widespread concern about possible disclosure of personal information.

The importance of this issue is reinforced by McGuire et al. (1994) who surveyed thirty secondary students engaged in a central Florida drug and alchohol treatment program. These authors reported that adolescent opinion favored more confidentiality than they expected to receive. Similarly, Remley and Albright's (1988) interview study carried out in a small adolescent sample across Virginia, Maryland, and Washington, D.C. concluded that not only were students confused about their counselor's purpose, but they did not feel that interviews would be kept confidential.

Eisenberg (1983) concluded that there were numerous indications in the literature that adolescents, like adults, are reluctant to seek help. For example, Nadler and Porat (1978) found that when adolescents' identity was known, they were unlikely to ask for assistance even on a straightforward general knowledge task. This finding seems likely to have implications for U.K. schools, since student identity and attendance are individually registered, and the latter parameter is monitored twice a day. Walster and Walster (1978) also found that adolescents tended to avoid adult help where a peer-support option was available.

In addition, Barnett et al. (1987) ascertained that adolescents were able to offer numerous reasons for not wanting to contact official channels of support, and Johnson et al. (1986) have pointed out that only rarely do adolescents request help. Moreover, this is an observation which has been found to be applicable even when young people have been distressed (Adelman & Taylor 1986; Whitaker et al. 1990). Eisenberg (1983) asserts that children, like adults, frequently respond negatively to aid from others and remain reluctant to seek help. Compared to younger children, the adolescent age group, it is suggested, becomes more negatively sensitive to help that implies dependent or incompetent behavior on their part and to help that creates an unwarranted sense of indebtedness toward the helping agent.

The acceptability of helping resources may also be related to professional perceptions of adolescents. For example, Jones and Nisbett (1971) have asserted that professional helpers often view adolescent problems as deriving largely from individual personality characteristics. Medway (1979) has also suggested that pupil's problems are believed by teachers to be produced by factors residing within the student, rather than by variables operating in the environment. Adelman and Taylor (1986) cite ten studies supporting the view that psychology and education professionals mistrust explanations and decisions offered by their clients. Moreover, Adelman and Taylor (1986) have argued that professionals often believe minors lack the competence to make informed judgments in their own best interests. These findings suggest the possibility that communication of negative helper attitudes may influence adolescent decisions to avoid getting help in school.

It has been similarly been suggested that reluctance is related to a lack of confidence in the treatment process (Baumrind 1978). Reluctance is also held to be a reaction against authority (Miller & Burt 1982). The psychoanalytic explanation is that reluctance to engage in treatment constitutes a defensive reaction against facing up to personal problems (Amanant 1979; Kaplan 1980; Wachtel 1982). Reluctance may also be related to a finding of Simoni, Adelman, and Perry (1991) that students expect professionals to offer a predominantly intellectual form of help, based upon adult evaluations of the quality of adolescent thinking. This concern should be taken seriously, given the current popularity of cognitive–behavioral interventions.

Despite the apparent variety of these suggestions, Adelman and Taylor (1986) argue that they share the characteristic of professional workers ignoring the possibility that a young person's reluctance may be appropriate to negative features of the potential intervention. Notably, some studies suggest that progress is poorer when participation has not been voluntary (Kopel & Arkowitz 1975;

Wilson 1979). Adelman and Taylor also point out that intervention for minors is frequently mandated by adults. Indeed, 30 percent of their adolescent sample indicated that they had been given no choice, and a further 21 percent reported negative perceptions of professional intervention. These included being asked too many questions, feeling pressured, and believing that receiving help might actually cause them more problems.

Adelman and Taylor (1986) assert that the reluctance of a significant number of minors is not inappropriately motivated, and therefore need not necessarily imply underlying pathology or skill deficiencies. These authors also argue that although actions designed to avoid treatment may appear deviant, this is not a sufficient basis for the diagnosis of emotional disturbance, learned helplessness, or learning difficulties, nor for prescriptive treatment interventions. They accordingly suggest that adolescent avoidance behaviors may not be evidence of irrationality, a valid symptom of pathology or skill deficiency, or inappropriate motivation. It was concluded that concepts about reluctance which emphasize only the deficiencies of children have severely restricted the focus of research, since minors are not a homogenous group.

SYNOPSIS OF RESEARCH ON VIEWS OF HELP RECEIVED

Studies on the Influence of Student Perception

From the evidence reviewed above, most studies suggest that the majority of students report that they derived benefit from professional support and were satisfied with the level of service received. From a consumer perspective the issues of significance are quite different from those of counselors, researchers, or observers, with an emphasis on quality of relationship rather than upon technical virtuosity or theoretical purity. While this body of research, like any other, is subject to certain methodological limitations, what remains impressive are findings that restate the importance of client perception in the helping process. Indeed, there is little to suggest that Gurman's (1977) conclusion, that client perception is a powerful concomitant of change, needs to be altered, regardless of the theoretical background of the professional helper.

Studies on the Influence of Student Preferences

From the available research, which is based almost entirely upon survey techniques, some promising hints on the preferences of secondary school students emerge. These include a leaning toward helpers who work a lot with students (Wiggins & Moody 1987), who are available, reliable, and supportive (De Weerdt 1986), who focus warmly on the students' needs from the start and encourage individual autonomy (Taylor, Adelman, & Kayser-Boyd 1986) and who cover the issues in not more than five sessions (Wiggins & Moody 1987).

While four studies highlight counselors as favored consultants in times of trouble (Gray 1980; Murray & Thompson 1985; Sproles 1988; Lehmanowsky 1991), three nominate teachers (Gray 1980; De Weerdt 1986; Sproles 1988) and two cite parents (Gray 1980; Sproles 1988) as adolescent-approved sources of help. Evidence on problems covered is very sparse from this area of research, but educational problems, social relationship issues, and alchohol or drug-related concerns accounted for 65 percent, 52 percent, and just over 20 percent of the problem total in the single study that was found to provide this type of information (Morey et al. 1989).

Studies on the Influence of Student Age

Age has emerged as a significant variable in four retrospective studies of adolescents' opinions of counseling. Students in their second year of secondary education tended to make more frequent use of counseling services (Morey et al. 1989), while Sinha (1972) found lower disclosure levels in fifteen and sixteen year olds than in peers two or three years younger. Northman (1985) noted that as students got older, they appeared to become more aware of the potential usefulness of help from others. In an earlier investigation, Northman (1978) had also observed that high school students preferred helpers who were either of their own age or a few years older.

Studies on the Influence of Student Gender

Following counselor intervention, females have been shown as more likely to say that they would seek help (De Paulo 1978b). In the study conducted by Newport (1977), three times more female students than male students stated that they had made contact with a school counselor. A higher frequency of female referral may be a relatively stable gender difference, since female students also report making more use of peer counselors (Morey et al. 1989). Females also perceive counselors as being more useful (Northman 1985); engage in greater self-disclosure in all-female counseling groups (Kraft & Vraa 1975); and rate residential drug-treatment programs more positively (Friedman, Glickman, & Kovach 1986).

Female students were not the predominant group without exception, however. In the Newport (1977) study, males formed the largest proportion in one category of respondents. Here, teachers initiated mandatory referral to counselors for 22 percent of male students (which was double the level for females), 44 percent of whom felt that the outcome had been purely disciplinary. In another variation on the reported gender findings, De Paulo (1978a) indicated that high school students also seem to prefer female helpers in situations which they consider serious. As far as adolescent levels of satisfaction are concerned however, neither gender nor age variables were found to exercise any significant effect (Morey et al. 1989).

Studies on the Influence of Student Culture

Cultural influences received attention in three of the above investigations. Dutch secondary students, against the overall trend for this group of posthelping studies, demonstrated favorable attitudes toward counseling for personal problems (De Weerdt 1986). Similarly, 50 percent of the Austrian adolescents in Seifert's (1985) survey indicated a need for increased counseling on personal concerns. In relation to student satisfaction data, however, Engen, Laing, and Sawyer (1988) reported that culture exercised no significant effects.

CONCLUSION

It would clearly be inaccurate to regard adolescence as a phase of human development devoid of demands upon and challenges to the individual's resources. It is therefore understandable that young people commonly seek support from others, and that they sometimes request professional help. Nonetheless, while some compensation may be found in more frequent adolescent support seeking for educational or career issues, the relatively low take-up rates for help with personal problems may be disappointing for teachers and school counselors who want to make this form of support available.

It seems possible that informal relationships in school may offer students sufficient support for low-level difficulties to render requests for teacher assistance unnecessary. Perhaps the low rates of seeking support for personal problems in school may also appear more understandable when viewed in the context of a developmental period which does not generally favor contact with professionals. From such little data as there are available, it seems likely that around one in five adolescents may experience problems acute enough to seek the assistance of a professional helper in school. However, a current constraint is that it remains unclear how far this estimate applies to students in English secondary schools, and there are additional restrictions upon current knowledge.

Even a cursory examination of the literature indicates that investigation of the perceptions of secondary age children represents an area of growing research interest. This may create an impression that by now a great deal is known about relevant adolescent experience and that such knowledge is securely founded. A detailed inspection of published research reports suggests, however, that this may not entirely be the case. Indeed, there appears to be a number of sampling and procedural shortcomings.

Among the studies reviewed, 38 percent of the samples were restricted, unrepresentative, unbalanced, or poorly described. Moreover, only 26 percent of the investigators reported that they had employed some process of randomization in setting up their research sample. It may be that more had done so in practice, but if so, in writing up their research, they omitted to record their action. Similarly, just 10 percent of the authors recorded that they had advised their sample that responses would be kept anonymous, while a mere 4 percent noted that the administration of research instruments had been carefully controlled. This characteristic of the reports is a matter of some importance, because perhaps the most consistent feature of this body of research was a lack of information regarding the readability of material presented to the students. Given that adolescent samples are likely to contain a substantial proportion of students with reading disabilities, this must be regarded as a significant omission, since most of the studies were carried out within school settings.

There are further limitations to be considered. Another aspect of equal importance is that the quality of descriptive protocols provided for other researchers was often less than satisfactory. In 36 percent of the studies reviewed, researchers failed to describe the procedure at a level of detail which would enable other workers to judge whether they could repeat the study. In 10 percent of the reports, the experimental protocol appeared to have been compromised by the adoption of differential information-gathering procedures across groups, for example, in variations of approach or time scale. Finally, 19 percent of the investigations were single-site studies, carried out with a small school or clinic sample, thereby limiting the extent to which the results might be applicable to other settings. The overall impression was that, in a high proportion of cases, some important aspect of the research lacked careful control. For all of the above reasons, due caution should be exercised before developing global conclusions from the results reported.

4

New Research Findings

These characteristics are not limited to demographics, or data that describes general attributes of participants in a study (such as numbers of males or females and their average ages) but include attributes of psychological significance.

Wakefield 1996, 648

Several reasons exist to explain why there is a need for new research carried out with English secondary school students. First, most existing work has been carried out in other countries, with unknown validity for English adolescents. Second, although two studies (Murgatroyd 1977; Hooper 1978) have previously looked into students' perceptions of help provided in English secondary schools, the fieldwork for these studies was done almost two decades ago, well before the advent of the National Curriculum, and represents only a single-site investigation paradigm. Third, it also appears that the research on school-based helping has not systematically examined process variables from an adolescent viewpoint. For these and other reasons, the development of new research efforts would now seem desirable.

To overcome some of the weaknesses in methodology apparent in previous studies (for a detailed technical specification, see Branwhite 1996), the research design presented here includes the following features:

- A multiple-site investigation in English secondary schools.
- A large-scale sample of students of differing ages.
- Application of a stratified random sampling procedure.
- Equal numbers of male and female students.
- Student-derived questionnaire content.
- Controlled readability instrumentation.
- Systematic questionnaire administration.
- Anonymity of student responding.
- Use of a range of statistical techniques.

Four research questions have particular relevance in considering the relevant areas of need among secondary school students.

1. How do students view their own approach to solving personal problems?
2. How do they perceive the helping resources of their school?
3. What are their preferences in helping situations?
4. What is their experience of getting help in school?

Clearly, each of these questions is important, and responses to all four can throw light upon adolescent experience prior to, during, or after initiation of the helping process. Information of this kind has the potential to fill some of the gaps in previous research, and it may also help to inform developments in professional practice, especially when the data are drawn from a general population cohort (as is the case in this study), thereby avoiding some of the limitations inherent in work attempted with a clinic sample.

FIELDWORK PROCEDURE

To obtain answers to the above questions, a twelve-step survey development plan was carried out with fifty secondary school students thirteen to sixteen years of age. This generated a forty-one-item multiple-choice questionnaire, color-coded into four sections, each of which contained student-focused items relating to one of the research questions. (An example of the completed questionnaire is included for your information in the appendix of this text.) Following administration of the completed questionnaire, the reported results were derived from a stratified random sample of 540 students (with equal numbers of male and female students in years eight, nine, and ten, averaging 14.4 years of age) attending six English secondary schools, three serving urban and three serving rural populations.

The collated data were analyzed using the Statistical Package for the Social Sciences (SPSS 1994). Techniques employed in the data analysis included descriptive statistics (means, ranges, and standard deviations), chi-square, Spearman's rank-order correlation, student's t, analysis of variance, and linear regression analysis. For readers interested in specific research design issues, a detailed technical specification of all the procedures employed for development, sampling, administration and data analysis purposes can be found in Branwhite (1996). To enhance readability in the outline that follows, the discussion is generally limited to the main survey findings and to statistical values at or beyond the 0.01 level of significance. Within the text, percentages have been rounded up or down to the nearest whole number for the same reason.

QUESTIONNAIRE RESULTS PART ONE: PERSONAL DETAILS

Preferred Social Context

Items in this part of the questionnaire set out to probe adolescents' preferred social context and their self-perceptions in the face of personal problems. The opening item asked students how they most liked to spend their time, in order to gain information about the context within which personal problems were likely to receive attention. In response, a large majority (74%) of the random sample indicated that they preferred to spend time with their friends. Just under 16 percent demonstrated a preference for spending time with their family, making peers by far the most popular focus of affiliation. Only 5 percent stated that they preferred to spend their time alone.

Number of Personal Problems

While 10 percent of the respondents indicated that they had a lot of personal problems, 85 percent opined that they had few or no problems. Consequently, data on the number of problems identified as likely topics for help were extracted to verify the general perception of having a small number of problems. The average for the sample worked out at almost four personal problems per student, within a reported range of zero to eleven problems, as can be seen from the related distribution (see Figure 4.1).

This array confirms that most students identified few problems that they would be likely to need help with. Indeed, a striking feature of the distribution is that it is skewed in that direction. Inspection of the above data also reveals that 81 percent of the

Figure 4.1
Percentage of Students Reporting a Given Number of Problems

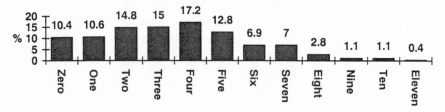

Range of Problems Indicated

Note: Percentage levels show proportion of sample responding for each item.

respondents fell within the range of zero to five problems, and 19 percent identified six to eleven problems, so that a relatively high number of problems appeared uncommon. Moreover, 60 percent of these secondary students indicated a moderate level of between two and five problems as potential targets for help.

Coping Responses

Virtually 38 percent of the sample recorded that they initially reacted to a personal problem by worrying about it. However, 21 percent told themselves that the situation could have been worse, and 14 percent said that they thought about something else. Only 10 percent indicated that their first reaction included getting angry, 4 percent reported that they laughed about the problem, and 3 percent admitted to crying. Subsequent coping strategies included trying to solve the problem independently (53%); asking someone else to help them to solve it (31%); or asking someone else to solve the problem for them (2%). Just 8 percent indicated that they did nothing.

Likely Problems for Help

Informative though this approach to personal problems may be, it provides no information about the type of problems that students had in mind. Specific issues which these secondary students predicted as likely topics for help from someone else are therefore displayed by order of magnitude (see Figure 4.2).

Although this sample is made up of students who are substantially below the statutory school-leaving age of sixteen years old,

Figure 4.2
Problem Areas for Which Help Was Deemed Likely to Be Necessary

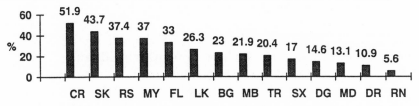

CR = CAREER	SK = SCHOOLWORK	RS = RELATIONSHIPS	MY = MONEY
FL = FEELINGS	LK = MY LOOKS	BG = BULLYING	MB = MY BODY
TR = TEACHERS	SX = SEX	DG = DRUGS	MD = MY MIND
DR = DREAMS	RN = RELIGION		

Note: Percentage levels show proportion of sample responding for each item.

many clearly have an eye to their own futures. The largest proportion of students (52%) indicated that help with careers was most likely to be sought. Schoolwork was also a salient issue for 44 percent of the sample. Therefore, it appears that a considerable proportion of those who by definition do not exhibit major academic problems consider themselves likely to require further help with their studies.

Over one-third (37%) of this multischool sample specified help with their relationships as a likely area of need. For a virtually equal percentage of the students, money was also identified as a topic for which they were likely to need support. A comparable 33 percent responded that their feelings were included among the topics for help in school, and 26 percent of the sample thought that they would need help regarding their looks, a concern which may have both physical and social implications.

Interestingly, 23 percent of this random sample reported that they would be likely to need help with the issue of bullying. Following the growing recent publicity attached to the existence and nature of bullying in the U.K. school system, it is only to be expected that at least some of the students would mention this topic as one of their concerns. It would also follow that adolescents might be expected to seek support regarding bullying. Hence it is encouraging to find some corroboration of these views within the survey data.

Some 20 percent suggested that they might require help regarding problems concerning teachers, although the precise nature of these problems was not specified.

Evidence of physically based concerns was further suggested by the 22 percent of these adolescents who indicated having some need for help with problems which were body related, and 17 percent who identified sex as a potential topic for help. The latter items suggest that there may be a cluster of adolescent concerns associated with puberty and sexual behavior. Despite some recent public alarm regarding adolescent substance abuse, only 15 percent of the sample reported a likely need for help with drug use. Neither did student concern regarding their own mental functioning feature prominently in the findings. Only a minority associated topics such as their mind (13%), dreams (11%), or religion (6%) with a potential need for help.

Independent Solutions

To conclude the overall findings for part one of the questionnaire, over one-half of the students (54%) reported that they had solved some personal problems without help, and 17 percent reported that they had solved a lot without help. On the other hand, only 15 percent said that they had solved a few problems, and a mere 5 percent indicated that they had solved no problems for themselves.

QUESTIONNAIRE RESULTS PART TWO: SCHOOL INFORMATION

Awareness and Choice of Helper

Part two of the questionnaire sought information on students' perceptions of the helping resources available in school. Just over a half of the sample (53%) responded "yes" when asked if it was possible to get help with personal problems in school. The remainder either indicated that help was not available or seemed unaware of its existence. Even greater disparity became apparent in student choice of a helper. Secondary students in this sample reported considerable diversity of opinion regarding their helper preferences, as Figure 4.3 demonstrates.

Virtually 25 percent of the students identified their form tutor (the teacher seen twice daily for registration, among other things) and virtually the same proportion identified someone else (a member of the school staff who was not one of the designated teachers). A differential scale of support for other teaching staff followed. In

Figure 4.3
Choice of Professional Helper in School

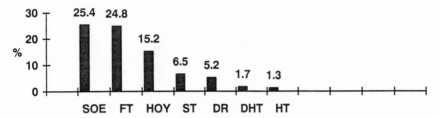

SOE = SOMEONE ELSE   HOY = HEAD OF YEAR   DHT = DEPUTY HEAD

FT = FORM TUTOR   ST = SUBJECT TEACHER   HT = HEADTEACHER

DR = DOCTOR

Note: Percentage levels show proportion of sample responding for each item.

comparison, 15 percent opted for their head of year, 7 percent identified a subject teacher, 2 percent selected their deputy head, and
just 1 percent their headteacher, the overall manager and authority figure in the school. A common thread running across these
members of the teaching staff is the relative infrequency of contact
which most students have with them compared to the connection
maintained by a form tutor.

While the same constraint holds true for doctors, they enjoy a
long-standing reputation as helpers, and this may go some way
toward accounting for the marginally higher number of students
(5%) who indicated that they would approach a doctor for help.
However, this still means that nineteen out of twenty students in
this secondary sample would not do so.

Use of Resources for Help in School

How are students likely to engage themselves with school-based
resources for helping out with personal problems? Important indications emerge from the set of data in Figure 4.4.

Whatever their choice of helper, this data shows that virtually
65 percent of the sample felt that access to their chosen helper was
easy or very easy, suggesting that the preferred adult maintained
a possibility of contact for them. As to the issue of how much of a
delay students would accept in receiving help, just above one-half

Figure 4.4
Use of Help Resources

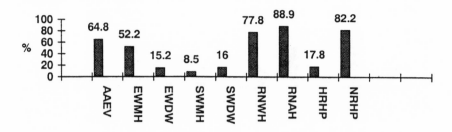

AAEV = ADULT ACCESS EASY/VERY EASY   EWMH = EXPECTED WAIT OF MINUTES OR HOURS

EWDW = EXPECTED WAIT OF DAYS OR WEEKS   SWMH = STUDENT WAITED MINUTES OR HOURS

SWDW = STUDENT WAITED DAYS OR WEEKS   HRHP = HAD RECEIVED HELP WITH PROBLEM

RNWH = RARELY/NEVER WANTED HELP   NRHP = NOT RECEIVED HELP WITH PROBLEM

RNAH = RARELY/NEVER ASKED FOR HELP

Note: Percentage levels show proportion of sample responding for each item.

of the sample (52%) indicated that they would expect to wait minutes or hours (and minutes were selected more than twice as often as hours), while only 15 percent checked days or weeks. Where students had referred a problem to a helper in school, however, 9 percent had waited minutes or hours before asking for help, while 16 percent had delayed for days or weeks.

There remains an open question as to whether young adolescents would seek help in school, since as far as personal problems were concerned, 78 percent stated that they had rarely or never wanted teacher assistance. Moreover, this attitudinal set appeared to be reflected in reported behavior, given that 89 percent responded that they had rarely or never asked for help. Hence minimal teacher consultation regarding personal problems was recorded by almost nine students in every ten surveyed.

To complete the emerging picture of widespread student avoidance of teacher consultation, part two of the questionnaire ended by requesting that respondents indicate whether they had actually received help in school, yielding an 18 percent return rate of "yes" responses, with 82 percent saying "no" to this item. That is, even though a substantial minority had received help from their teachers, the incidence of positive to negative responses occurred in the ratio of almost 1:4, reiterating the point that receipt of teacher assistance was highly selective for the majority of the student sample.

QUESTIONNAIRE RESULTS PART THREE: PERSONAL PREFERENCES

Preferred Helper Characteristics

Findings for this part of the questionnaire are reported as a percentage of the 444 students who responded in Part Two that they had *not* received teacher assistance with a personal problem. The data reported in Figure 4.5 therefore relate to student preferences regarding potential helpers.

The data show which particular attributes most of the students regarded as important in identifying others as potential helpers. Well over one-half of the sample (57%) identified friends the most popular choice of helper. With another 25 percent indicating that they would prefer one of their own parents, students appeared to favor well-known informal helpers. This impression is enhanced by the fact that choices indicating a friend's parent, someone else, another professional, a teacher, or another student were all supported by less than 5 percent of the sample.

Figure 4.5
Preferred Helper Attributes and Identity

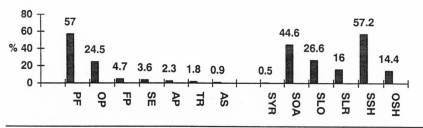

PF = PERSONAL FRIEND   OP = OWN PARENT   SYR = SOMEONE YOUNGER

FP = FRIEND'S PARENT   SE = SOMEONE ELSE   SOA = SOMEONE YOUR OWN AGE

AP = ANOTHER PROFESSIONAL TR = TEACHER   SLO = SOMEONE A LITTLE OLDER

AS = ANOTHER STUDENT   SLR = SOMEONE A LOT OLDER

                                                SSH = SAME-SEX HELPER

                                                OSH = OTHER-SEX HELPER

Note: Percentage levels show proportion of sample responding for each item.

One variable influencing the popularity of friends may be that of chronological age. The importance of age as a qualifying variable is reinforced by the finding that 45 percent of the students stated a preference for a helper of their own age, perhaps because of an increased likelihood of maximizing common experience. By way of contrast, less than 1 percent stated a preference for someone younger, while 26 percent opted for someone a little older, and a smaller set of 16 percent favored someone a lot older. Therefore an exact match of ages may not be the most relevant factor, since it appears that 43 percent of those responding would accept an older helper, even though this was not the model choice. Nonetheless, age proximity seems to be important, given that 72 percent of the students preferred a helper no more than a little older than themselves.

Influential though it appears to be, age is clearly not the only important variable affecting choice of helper during early adolescence. In this sample of students, parents received twelve times more support as potential helpers than did teachers. Therefore, while helper age may render some adult helpers unattractive in a school setting, outside of school this finding may be altered by family variables. There is another notable exception to the hypothesis that age operates as the critical feature in choosing a helper. Figure 4.5 shows in addition helper sex was considered meaningful. The students' response demonstrated that although 57 percent preferred a same-sex helper, only 14 percent favored a helper of the opposite sex. That is, the ratio of students wanting a same-sex helper to an opposite-sex helper was just over 4:1. Hence a model helper for the majority of these adolescents might well take the form a friend of their own age and own sex.

Referral and Helper Contact Preferences

All the six schools involved in this study (in common with many U.K. secondary schools) actually had conventional teacher-resourced pastoral care programs in place. A primary consideration was therefore how students might seek teacher support when they had a personal problem. Figure 4.6 provides information germane to the issue of what early adolescents would prefer if they *had* to consult with a teacher.

With 74 percent of the students responding that they would prefer a teacher to find out about their problem directly from themselves, these secondary school students reflected a high level of personal responsibility for handling their problems. Even the option of having a friend contact the helper was selected by only 7 percent of the sample, and the alternative of having the family do it was favored by a mere 5 percent. Notably, the very common path-

Figure 4.6
Referral and Helper Contact Preferences

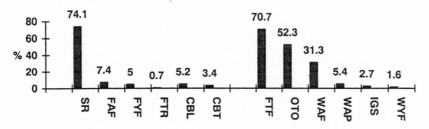

SR = SELF-REFERRAL   FAF = FROM A FRIEND   FTF = FACE-TO-FACE MEETING

FYF = FROM YOUR FAMILY   FTR = FROM A TEACHER   OTO = ONE-TO-ONE MEETING

CBL = CONTACT BY LETTER CBT = CONTACT BY TELEPHONE   WAF = WITH A FRIEND

WAP = WITH A PARENT

IGS = IN A GROUP OF STUDENTS

WYF = WITH YOUR FAMILY

Note: Percentage levels show proportion of sample responding for each item.

way of teacher-initiated referral was favored by less than 1 percent of these adolescents. Personal contact was much more strongly endorsed than contact by letter or by telephone.

In addition, a reassuring level of coping is implicit in the finding that 71 percent of this group of students wanted a face-to-face meeting, in contrast to 3 percent stating a preference for telephone contact. Moreover, 52 percent of these teenagers wanted to enter into any postreferral meeting alone (i.e., just themselves with the teacher concerned), although another 31 percent said that they would rather have a friend present at that juncture. Only 5 percent wanted a parent to be present, and just under 2 percent wished their whole family to be there. Just below 3 percent of the students indicated a preference for meeting a helper in a group of students experiencing problems.

Meeting Time and Location Preferences

Adults may assume that young adolescents find professional priorities regarding the time and place of meetings all equally attractive, and Figure 4.7 provides information that bears on this issue.

Figure 4.7
Time and Location Preferences

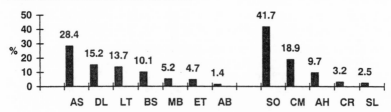

AS = AFTER SCHOOL   DL = DURING LESSONS   SO = SCHOOL OFFICE CM = CLASSROOM

LT = LUNCHTIME   BS = BEFORE SCHOOL   AH = AT HOME   CR = IN A CORRIDOR

MB = MORNING BREAK ET = EVENING TIME   SL = SCHOOL LIBRARY

AB = AFTERNOON BREAK

Note: Percentage levels show proportion of sample responding for each item.

The strongest category of response involved 28 percent of the respondents, who chose an after school meeting as their personal preference. There was less support for meeting during lessons, with 15 percent deciding on this option. Lunchtime meetings were favored by only 14 percent of the students. Taken overall, 36 percent of the sample stated a preference for a meeting during the school day, 39 percent for a meeting during the day but outside of school hours, with only 5 percent favoring an evening meeting.

Offered a variety of possible venues to choose from, the favorite meeting place turned out to be in a school office for 42 percent of the students. In comparison, 19 percent opted for a classroom, and 10 percent for their home. School corridors or the library were almost universally out of favor (receiving support from 3% and 2%, respectively). One feature common to classroom, corridor, and library options is that of the increased risk of individual exposure to observation by others, notably peers, which may go some way toward explaining why they were less popular choices.

Helper Communication Preferences

Much of the assistance potentially available from adult helpers in the school system is mediated through a process of verbal communication, and consequently adolescent opinion on this process is of considerable interest, since it may offer a formative input which can contribute toward enhanced helper effectiveness, as is portrayed in Figure 4.8.

By far the greatest proportion of these young adolescents expressed a desire for the person helping them to communicate in an active and problem-sensitive manner. When asked how they would like a helper to assist them to start talking, 56 percent of the sample indicated that they should be asked what was the matter. Interestingly, less than half this number (26%) was concerned about being called by their first name, suggesting that it is the nature of the problem which is the more widespread concern.

To gain assistance in describing a personal problem, 43 percent of the students wanted to be asked specifically to talk about it, compared with only 18 percent who simply wanted to be asked if they had a problem. Another 39 percent indicated that they would like to be asked questions about their problem. Developing a pool of information about the problem may therefore be considered an important task to be accomplished during the helping intervention with adolescent students.

Help with describing feelings, a topic almost universally thought by professionals to be crucial in providing help, was also consid-

Figure 4.8
Helper Communication Preferences

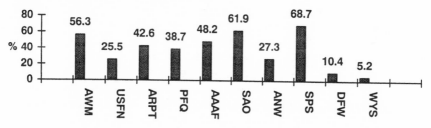

AWM = ASK WHAT IS THE MATTER	USFN = USE OF STUDENT'S FIRST NAME
ARPT = ADULT REQUESTS PROBLEM TALK	PFQ = PROBLEM-FOCUSSED QUESTIONS
AAAF = ADULT ASKS ABOUT FEELINGS	SAO = SUGGEST ALTERNATIVE OPTIONS
ANW = BE ADVISED NOT TO WORRY	SPS = SUGGEST POSSIBLE SOLUTIONS
DFW = DESCRIBE PROBLEM IN A FEW WORDS	WYS = WAIT FOR STUDENT TO SPEAK

Note: Percentage levels show proportion of sample responding for each item.

ered important for this teenage sample. Indeed their views were stacked in a similar hierarchy to that derived for talking about the problem. That is, 48 percent wanted to be asked how they felt, 30 percent preferred that a helper should ask questions about their feelings, and an additional 23 percent indicated a desire to be asked if they had told anyone else about their feelings.

It is a matter of some interest that by far the most strongly supported helper action for developing student options (supported by 62% of the sample) was to give some suggestions. A further 27 percent also wanted to be told not to worry, an outcome probably related to the part one finding: that of six potential reactions to a personal problem, worrying, (a form of cognition involving self-statements of anxiety, inability to cope, and other negatively loaded causal attributions) was reported by the greatest number of survey respondents.

Likewise, in formulating steps toward resolving a problem, 69 percent of those responding indicated that they would like helpers to suggest a solution. Another 20 percent also wanted to be asked if they knew of a possible solution themselves. Just 10 percent of the sample stated that they would like a helper to describe their problem in a few words. Furthermore, only 5 percent wanted a helper to wait for them to speak first, suggesting that the notion of shared silence may not hold high validity for students of secondary age.

Predicted Reasons for Terminating Contact

The likely reasons why adolescents may terminate contact with a helper form another important professional consideration in secondary schools, and these are outlined in Figure 4.9.

Almost 47 percent of the sample stated that they would stop seeing an adult helper who told someone else what they had said, suggesting that trust is an important issue for this age group. Another 39 percent added that they would terminate contact if their helper asked questions that were too personal, and 19 percent cited being asked too many questions, so that some students may be sensitive to perceptions of being interrogated. It is of equal interest, however, that almost an identical proportion of the student sample (39%) cited the problem stopping as another reason for breaking off contact with a helper in school, an outcome which reiterates the problem focus of adolescent help-seeking behavior. Being given either too much or too little help were additional reasons for terminating contact, options which were checked by 18 percent and 5 percent of the sample, respectively.

Figure 4.9
Predicted Reasons for Terminating Contact

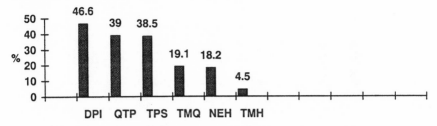

DPI = DISCLOSING PERSONAL INFORMATION TMQ = TOO MANY QUESTIONS ASKED

QTP = QUESTIONS TOO PERSONAL NEH = NOT ENOUGH HELP GIVEN

TPS = PROBLEM STOPPED TMH = TOO MUCH HELP GIVEN

Note: Percentage levels show proportion of sample responding for each item.

Recommendation to School Friends

An alternative index of what students value in helping contexts is shown in Figure 4.10, which displays choices relating to the advice that they would *first* offer to a school friend with a personal problem.

The hierarchy of preferences for the first three items of Figure 4.10 provides the greatest level support for friends and parents as sources of assistance with personal problems, an outcome which provides cross-validation for the same trend in Figure 4.5. The percentage favoring the friend option is markedly lower, however (30% versus 57% in Figure 4.5) reducing the number of students stating this preference by almost one-half. This suggests the possibility that self-interest may be influential in deciding what to do when faced with personal problems. While the level of support for parent assistance registers very little change in this table (28% compared with 25% for Figure 4.5), however, support for teacher assistance appears stronger (15% against 2% in Figure 4.5) when considering the needs of friends. This finding underlines the possibility that different motivations may influence adolescent thinking about teacher support for the self and for others.

Figure 4.10
Initial Recommendation to School Friends

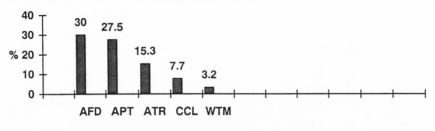

AFD = ASK A FRIEND   APT = ASK A PARENT   ATR = ASK A TEACHER

CCL = CALL CHILDLINE   WTM = WRITE TO A MAGAZINE

Note: Percentage levels show proportion of sample responding for each item.

QUESTIONNAIRE RESULTS PART FOUR:
EXPERIENCE OF TEACHER HELP

Rationale for Seeking Help

Part four of the questionnaire was completed by the 18 percent of the student sample who responded in part two that they *had* received teacher assistance with a personal problem. Findings for this part of the questionnaire are reported as a percentage of the randomly selected (N = 96) students responding. The adolescent mode of seeking teacher assistance with a personal problem is delineated in Figure 4.11.

Extending the findings from part one of the questionnaire, further evidence emerges of secondary students' inclination to take personal responsibility for their problems, since almost 46 percent indicated that they decided to seek help of their own volition. A further 24 percent of the sample stated that they did so because a friend said they should, and another 22 percent took this action on the basis of parental advice. Referral on the basis of teacher recommendation was undertaken by a mere 4 percent of the students. Consequently, the influence exercised by either friends or parents alone appears to be substantially more widespread in this age group (by a factor of five) than that of teachers. When taken together, friend and parent-initiated referrals accounted for virtually 46 percent of the total, almost identical with the level of support for self-referral, which was the single most influential variable.

Figure 4.11
Rationale for Self-Referral

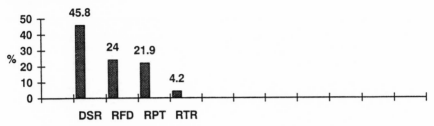

DSR = DECISION TO SELF-REFER   RFD = RECOMMENDATION OF A FRIEND

RPT = RECOMMENDATION OF A PARENT   RTR = RECOMMENDATION OF A TEACHER

Note: Percentage levels show proportion of sample responding for each item.

Experience of Teacher Attention

The adolescent perspective on what happens when they are in receipt of help with personal problems is likely to be of value in considering how to make such interventions more effective, and the next two figures provide data which bear directly on this important issue. Strategies for building rapport are essential for developing the contact between student and helper, and this is the area addressed first. However, it should be noted that because Figures 4.12 and 4.13 reflect the order of events likely to be encountered in the helping process, they do not therefore list the data in order of magnitude.

We can note that 44 percent of the sample recorded that teachers looked at them, 29 percent reported that teachers greeted them, and 34 percent of the students said that they were called by their first name. A further 47 percent indicated that teachers had asked how they felt, and 40 percent that teachers had inquired whether they had told anyone else about their feelings. Close to 70 percent of the sample noted that they had been asked related questions.

In 34 percent of the instances, students stated that their teachers had looked interested, and 31 percent said that teachers had nodded their heads while they were talking to them. In addition, 56 percent had been told not to worry and just over one-half of the students (54%) recorded that teachers said they would help. Al-

Figure 4.12
Experience of Teacher Rapport

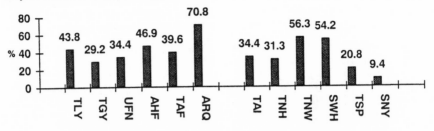

TLY = TEACHER LOOKED AT YOU   TAI = TEACHER APPEARED INTERESTED

TGY = TEACHER GREETED YOU   TNH = TEACHER NODDED THEIR HEAD

UFN = USED YOUR FIRST NAME   TNW = TOLD YOU NOT TO WORRY

AHF = ASKED HOW YOU FELT   SWH = SAID THEY WOULD HELP

TAF = ASKED IF YOU HAD TOLD ANYONE   TSP = TOLD YOU A SIMILAR PROBLEM

        ABOUT YOUR FEELINGS   OF THEIR OWN

ARQ = ASKED RELATED QUESTIONS   SNY = SAID SOMETHING NICE ABOUT YOU

Note: Percentage levels show proportion of sample responding for each item.

most 21 percent of the students indicated that teachers had told them about a similar problem of their own, and 9 percent reported that their teachers had said something nice about them.

Experience of the Helping Intervention

Apart from reporting the receipt of anxiety-reducing and reassuring comments from their helpers, secondary students also gave indications of having received the close attention to their problem that findings from part three suggest that they would want.

Virtually one-half of the responding adolescents attested to relevant problem-related support from their teacher, 51 percent in the form of requests to describe the problem, and 49 percent via problem-related questions. Only 13 percent reported that teachers had described their problem in a few words, which suggests that

Figure 4.13
Experience of the Problem Intervention

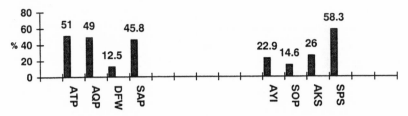

ATP = ASKED YOU TO TALK ABOUT THE PROBLEM   AYI = ASKED FOR YOUR IDEAS

AQP = ASKED YOU QUESTIONS ABOUT THE PROBLEM   SOP = ASKED HOW YOU HAD SOLVED

DFW= DESCRIBED YOUR PROBLEM IN A FEW WORDS   OTHER PROBLEMS

SAP = SUGGESTED ALTERNATIVES FOR HANDLING   AKS = ASKED IF YOU KNEW A SOLUTION

          THE PROBLEM   SPS = SUGGESTED A POSSIBLE SOLUTION

Note: Percentage levels show proportion of sample responding for each item.

attempts to paraphrase students' accounts of their difficulties were not common. However, 46 percent of the sample recorded that their teachers had suggested alternatives for handling the problem discussed. For 23 percent of those responding, teachers had asked for their ideas. Likewise, 15 percent inquired how they had solved other problems, and 26 percent asked if they knew of a solution for their current problem. More than double this number reported that teachers had suggested possible solutions.

Expectation and Evaluation of Help Received

Figure 4.14 provides an index of how far the help provided actually met with students' ideas of what might happen when they received help from a teacher.

When asked how much of the help that they had been given was the kind of help they expected, 15 percent of the students felt that all of the teacher assistance provided met expectations. When combined with the further 53 percent who reported that most of the help received had met this criterion, this shows that two-thirds of the sample had the majority of their expectations met, since the data in this table represent discrete groups of students. A further 23 percent indicated that a little of the help given was as they ex-

Figure 4.14
Student Expectations and Evaluation of Help Received

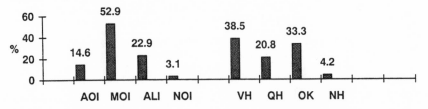

| MOI = MOST OF IT | ALI = A LITTLE OF IT | VH = VERY HELPFUL | QH = QUITE HELPFUL |
| AOI = ALL OF IT | NOI = NONE OF IT | OK = O.K. | NH = NOT HELPFUL |

Note: Percentage levels show proportion of sample responding for each item.

pected, but only a very small minority (3%) stated that none of it was. These findings suggest that some level of information regarding the helping process was available to students in the schools concerned prior to the time the assistance was received. It appears, however, that about one in four students did not see their expectations fulfilled.

Apart from the issue of whether the helping intervention was in accord with students' expectations, a further question probed for information on respondents' perceptions of the effectiveness of the help that they had received. Given that almost 39 percent evaluated teacher assistance as having been very helpful, marginally over 20 percent judged it as quite helpful, and an additional 33 percent rated the help provided as OK, it may be concluded that nine out of ten students in the sample believed that the help which they had been given was acceptable. Only a very small proportion (4%) actually rated the requested teacher assistance as not helpful.

Effects of the Intervention

No less important than the evaluation assigned by students to the help that they received is the issue of its after effects, and the relative index of opinion pertinent to this issue appears in Figure 4.15.

In order of magnitude, 38 percent of those who had received help from a teacher reported that the problem got better even if it did not go away altogether, and a further 29 percent found that it went away completely. Since these were discrete response categories, it

Figure 4.15
Effects of the Intervention

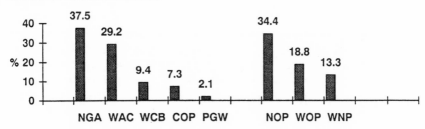

NGA = PROBLEM GOT BETTER BUT DID NOT GO AWAY

WAC = PROBLEM WENT AWAY COMPLETELY

WCB = PROBLEM WENT AWAY BUT CAME BACK

COP = PROBLEM CAUSED OTHER PROBLEMS

PGW = PROBLEM GOT WORSE

NOP = INTERVENTION DID NOT HELP

    WITH OTHER PROBLEMS

WOP = INTERVENTION HELPED WITH

    AN OLD PROBLEM

WNP = INTERVENTION HELPED WITH A

    NEW PROBLEM THAT STARTED

    SINCE YOU GOT HELP

Note: Percentage levels show proportion of sample responding for each item.

therefore follows that two-thirds of these students obtained some relief from their problem. For 9 percent, however, the original problem came back, for 7 percent it caused other problems, and for 2 percent it actually got worse. A related question was that of how far the help provided also assisted the students in coping with other problems. Here, 34 percent of those responding said that it did *not* help with other problems, 19 percent said that it helped with an *old* problem, and 13 percent indicated that it helped with a *new* problem. Hence, while one-third of the sample did not generalize the influence of the intervention, another one-third clearly did.

Topics Classed As Easy to Talk About

Respondents were also asked to indicate which topics they found easy to talk about and which topics they found hard. The results are displayed in Figures 4.16 and 4.17 in order of the magnitude of student support for each item.

Figure 4.16
Topics Retrospectively Classed As Easy to Talk About

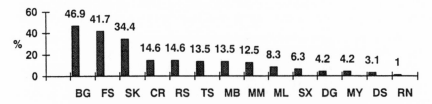

BG = BULLYING   FS = FEELINGS   SK = SCHOOLWORK   CR = CAREER

RS = RELATIONSHIPS   TS = TEACHERS   MB = MY BODY   MM = MY MIND

ML = MY LOOKS   SX = SEX   DG = DRUGS   MY = MONEY

DS = DREAMS   RN = RELIGION

Note: Percentage levels show proportion of sample responding for each item.

Figure 4.17
Topics Retrospectively Classed As Hard to Talk About

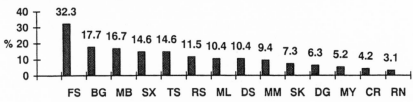

FS = FEELINGS   BG = BULLYING   MB = MY BODY   SX = SEX

TS = TEACHERS   RS = RELATIONSHIPS   ML = MY LOOKS   DS = DREAMS

MM = MY MIND   SK = SCHOOLWORK   DG = DRUGS   MY = MONEY

RN = RELIGION   CR = CAREER

Note: Percentage levels show proportion of sample responding for each item.

The easy topics may be differentiated into three main groups. The first of these includes talking about bullying, feelings, and schoolwork, all items supported by over one-third of the sample.

The second group included talking about career, relationships, teachers, body, and mind, items which were only poorly supported by between 13 percent and 15 percent of the students. The third group, assembling on the low end of the scale, and each accounting for less than 10 percent of the respondents, included talking about looks, sex, drugs, money, dreams, and religion. Hence it appears that issues of immediate personal value in the school setting are those which most of these secondary students found easy to discuss with their teachers.

Topics Classed As Hard to Talk About

The other half of this question concerns those issues which secondary students identified retrospectively as items which were hard to talk about, which might be expected to reveal a different picture.

This time it is apparent that only one item (my feelings) was identified by anything like one-third of the sample, compared with three such items in Figure 4.16. As in the previous figure, however, six items (though not the same six) were supported by less than 10 percent of the sample. An intermediate group of seven options (bullying, my body, sex, teachers, relationships, my looks, and dreams) were supported by 10 to 18 percent of those responding.

The logical prediction—that one of the preceding two figures should be the complete reverse of the other—is clearly not borne out by the data. Although the topics of feelings and bullying constituted the first two ranks in Figures 4.16 and 4.17, their positions reversed with regard to each other, and religion gained least support as an easy topic but also least support as a hard one. A significant difference in the overall rankings was nonetheless obtained ($p = <0.05$; 2-tailed test) using Spearman's rank-order correlation, with the largest item differences occurring for career, schoolwork, dreams, and sex.

SYNOPSIS OF MAIN SURVEY FINDINGS

Findings on Personal Details

Part one of this survey ($N = 540$) produced strongest support for the view that young to midadolescents prefer to spend time with their friends rather than with their family or alone. While the number of personal problems recorded ranged from zero to eleven, the majority of students reported having only a few personal problems that they would be likely to need help with. They tended to worry about such problems they did have, but nonetheless attempted to deal with these themselves; and reported that they had already solved some of their problems. Between 33 percent and 52 percent reported that they would be likely to need help with problems related to their career, schoolwork, relationships, money, and their feelings.

Findings on School Information

Part two of the survey (N = 540) indicated that most of the sample recognized that help was available in school, and among the identifiable adults would favor their form tutor as a helper. The vast majority of these secondary students indicated that they had neither wanted nor asked for help for personal problems in school, and accordingly, just over 80 percent of them recorded that they had not received such help, with 18 percent conversely stating that they had received help.

Findings on Personal Preferences

Part three findings (N = 444) highlighted a utilitarian helper profile as being one involving a personal friend of the same age and the same sex, and by comparison less than 4 percent of the respondents favored a professional helper. Most of the students said that they wanted to refer themselves to a helper, with less than 1 percent supporting referral by a teacher. A one-to-one, face-to-face meeting was the preferred mode of contact. Written or telephone contact received support from less than 7 percent of this group of adolescents. The single most popular time for meeting a helper was after school hours. Most of the sample wanted helpers to ask them about both their problems and their feelings. More notably, the options of assistance in working out their options and in creating possible solutions received particulary strong support. Termination of helper contact was most frequently predicted where another person was told about what students had said.

Findings on Experience of Getting Help

Part four outcomes (N = 96) reiterated that the strongest level of support (46%) was in favor of self-referral for help with personal problems in school. Most of those responding also indicated that the teacher providing assistance had not only asked about their problems and their feelings, but had also told them not to worry and that they would help. Moreover, the help offered had included suggesting some possible solutions to the referred problem. The greatest proportion of the sample (67%) additionally reported that all or most of the help given was in accord with what they expected; just over 90 percent rated the help as either OK, quite helpful, or very helpful; and for most students (67%) the problem with which they had been helped then got better. Less than 10 percent reported effects such as the problem getting worse or causing other problems. About one-third of these adolescents (32%) indicated that the help received had also assisted them with other problems. Topics classed as easy to talk about by 33 percent or more of the sample included bullying, feelings, and schoolwork, whereas a comparable level of nomination for hard topics was encountered only with respect to bullying.

To determine whether any particular main variable would be more effective than the others in predicting the results obtained, the data from age, sex, school, and location variables were analyzed using the SPSS linear regression function. This analysis yielded nonsignificant results. Therefore it appeared that no single main variable had contributed a significantly greater effect to the survey findings than had either of the others.

5

New Perspectives

The ways in which young people understand and perceive themselves, their own agency and personality, and their various social situations have a powerful effect on their subsequent reactions to various life events.

Coleman and Hendry 1990, 45

STUDY SCOPE AND SEQUENCE

As indicated in Chapter 4, each main research question was addressed through a separate part of the survey. In the discussion that follows, findings from each part are introduced via a representative student profile, derived from the modal number of responses made against items included in the relevant part of the questionnaire. In addition to reviewing the results of the present investigation, this discussion incorporates relevant findings from the international research literature.

SELF-REPORT ISSUES

The survey research described here is based upon self-report data. A brief comment on the value of self-report material seems warranted, since Eisenberg (1983) has expressed concern about the accuracy of self-reports, on the grounds that answers may be unduly influenced by social desirability. However, while in certain situations this might be regarded as a legitimate anxiety, such an assertion may not be universally applicable. Indeed, based upon their research into the perceptions of parents and adolescents in a general population sample, Verhulst and Van der Ende (1992) concluded that adolescents are indispensable informants on their own problem behaviors. Achenbach and Edelbrock (1987) have also demonstrated that self-reports from adolescents can be both valid and reliable.

Moreover, in the present study, students' answers were written anonymously under examination conditions, which were employed specifically to exercise control over social interaction and peer influence. The resulting self-report data are therefore considered to be less vulnerable to social desirability effects than those obtained through interview or group discussion. For these reasons, the data presented here are believed to provide a viable index of adolescent preferences and reported experience in help-seeking situations.

DISCUSSION OF THE PART ONE FINDINGS ON PERSONAL INFORMATION

STUDENT PROFILE ONE

A representative secondary school student prefers to spend his or her time with friends rather than with family, and in general thinks that he or she has few personal problems. Where problems exist that are likely to need help, however, in order of priority these most probably involve concerns about their career, schoolwork, relationships, money, feelings, or looks.

Recognizing that he or she has already solved some personal problems without help, the student's mode of coping with a further problem is likely to involve worrying about it initially and later endeavoring to create a solution for it independently. Accordingly, the student regards it as improbable that he or she would need help with any of the fourteen problem categories listed in part one of the questionnaire. Attempts to avoid a personal problem, laugh it off, or more emotive reactions such as getting angry or crying are in general very unlikely to be adopted.

Social Orientation

Providing information about the context in which adolescent problem solving seems likely to arise, in excess of 90 percent of the students reported that they preferred to spend their time in the company of others. Friends appear to be the primary source of adolescent affiliation, an option which was upheld despite differences in culture and the quarter of a century which has elapsed since this finding was reported by Wright and Keple (1981). Moreover, a preference for spending time with friends was indicated over four times more frequently than spending time with their own family and fourteen times more often than spending time alone. This pattern was unaffected by age or gender differences. On the basis of this preference hierarchy, it might be expected that secondary students commonly involve friends or parents (but particularly their friends) in addressing personal problems.

Number of Problems

Most students did not believe themselves to be overwhelmed with personal problems. There was no repeat of a peak in the perceived level of personal problems at around fourteen years of age reported by Porteous (1985). Indeed, no significant difference occurred on this variable in any year group. The divergence in findings may possibly derive from the inclusion of sixteen year olds in the Porteous study or to fluctuations in adolescent concerns during the intervening decade. Likewise, in the present research, no decrease was recorded in adolescent concerns across year groups to support the findings of Gallagher et al. (1992). Although that was a more recent investigation than the research of Porteous, it similarly included older adolescents (in the Gallagher et al. study, those up to eighteen years of age) and was carried out in Northern Ireland. The difference in results may consequently be due to variations between the studies concerned across age, cultural, or environmental factors.

Within the research reported here, there were significantly more females ($p < 0.01$) among those who indicated that they had a lot of problems. This result supports previous research by Caspar, Belanoff, and Offer (1996); Forehand, Neighbours, and Wierson (1991); Gallagher et al. (1992); McGee and Stanton (1992); and Offord et al. (1987). However, among those recording that they had no problems in the current study, there were significantly more males ($p < 0.01$), and this appears to be a new finding in the context of the literature reviewed.

With regard to the specific number of problems indicated, four times more students reported a range of zero to five problems than reported six to eleven problems. Hence the overall student perception of having few personal problems was empirically supported.

However, the relative frequencies also suggest that when adolescents do consider getting help, it is most unlikely that are concerned about only a single issue, since 79 percent reported that they would be likely to need assistance with more than one problem.

The number of problems differed significantly between the sexes (p < 0.001), being higher for females, but there was no such difference across year groups. The former result supports the findings of Stark et al. (1989) but the latter finding does not. This divergence may be explained by the inclusion of adolescents of sixteen and seventeen years in the Stark et al. study (older students made up just over one-third of their total sample).

Common Types of Problems

Of the problems identified as likely areas for help, the most common concerns for respondents (including between 33% and 52% of the sample) included their career, schoolwork, relationships, money, and feelings. The constellation of career, schoolwork, self, and relationship issues is buttressed by at least ten other studies.

Problems with a Career

Career issues have been identified consistently by adolescent respondents in the studies of Boldero and Fallon (1995); Friedman (1991); Gallagher et al. (1992); Gillies (1989); Hutchinson and Reagan (1989); Nurmi, Poole, and Kalakoski (1994); Porteous and Fisher (1980); Porteous and Kelleher (1987); and Violato and Holden (1988). In this context, Tyler (1964) has suggested that occupational concepts may generally not be formed prior to early adolescence. In the economic climate of today however, it appears that either they are now formed in the preadolescent years, or that such thinking comes to the fore during early adolescence.

Problems with Schoolwork

Concerns about schoolwork have also emerged repeatedly, as shown by the work of Adelman (1993); Esser et al. (1990); Friedman (1991); Gillies (1989); Hooper (1978); Hutchinson and Reagan (1989); Keys and Fernandes (1992); Kurdek (1987); Littrell, Malia, and Vanderwood (1995); Nurmi, Poole, and Kalakoski (1994); Porteous (1985); Spirito et al. (1991); Tabberer (1984); Violato and Holden (1988); and Yamamoto et al. (1987). The evidence of educational concerns represents one of the more perennial findings from self-report studies of adolescent problems.

Problems with the Self

Evidence of self-concern among these English teenagers (33% regarding their feelings, 26% with their looks, and 22% about their body) suggest that this may be a relatively widespread phenomenon. Adolescent unease about some aspect of their emotional or physical functioning has previously been recorded by Blum, McKay, Resnick, Geer, and Campbell (1989); Boldero and Fallon (1995); Chaudhari (1976); Collins and Harper (1974); Esser, Schmidt, and Woerner (1990); Friedman (1991); Gillies (1989); Gordon and Grant (1997); Kurdek (1987); Nurmi, Poole, and Kalakoski (1994); Porteous and Fisher (1980); and Violato and Holden (1988). Accordingly, it may be concluded that this inference receives substantive support from the literature.

Problems with Relationships

Problems with relationships are likewise widely attested to and are recorded by Adelman (1993); Armacost (1989); Boldero and Fallon (1995); Branwhite (1994); Collins and Harper (1974); Friedman (1991); Hooper (1978); Keys and Fernandes (1992); Kurdek (1987); Littrell, Malia, and Vanderwood (1985); McGee and Stanton (1992); Nurmi, Poole, and Kalakoski (1994); Porteous and Fisher (1980); Spirito et al. (1991); and Violato and Holden (1988). Perhaps the consistency of this finding is to be expected given the students' membership of peer group, friendship, family, and school-based systems, each of which may offer potential for interpersonal difficulties to occur.

Exceptions to the Common Types of Problems

Although there were instances in which the findings of this study received widespread empirical backing, in the present research there were some notable exceptions to the pattern of core problems with multiple-study support. Items within this group include those for which only a few supporting studies could be traced.

Problems with Money

For this variable, 37 percent of these English students cited money as a likely problem, and this has been little reported elsewhere. That proportion of respondents is over nine times higher than the 4 percent identified by McGee and Stanton (1992) in New Zealand. It is also over six times greater than the 6 percent described by

Morey et al. (1989) in the United States, and more than one-half as many again as the 24 percent reported by Gillies (1989) in Nottingham. It may perhaps be that this finding reflects cultural differences in student experience or perception. However, an increasing adolescent sense of financial pressure in recent years cannot altogether be ruled out and may derive from new marketing strategies designed to target potential adolescent consumers.

Problems with Bullying

Further divergence from the core of widely supported research results was implicit in the finding that 23 percent of the present sample identified bullying as a problem for which they would be likely to need help. This issue has also been less commonly reported. Anxieties focused on bullying have a shorter history of research investigation, and comparison with American research is inhibited by an apparent lack of traceable studies. However, the obtained level of student concern (23%) does not differ markedly from the 19 percent reported by Branwhite (1994) and the 18 percent recorded by Smith (1991) from previous studies carried out in English secondary schools.

Problems with Teachers

Marginally over 20 percent of the sample identified teachers as a problem with which they would be likely to need help. This is a much lower proportion than that occurring in the one other U.K. study found to report on this issue. Hooper (1978) recorded that 76 percent of his West of England sample reported problems with teachers. This difference may be attributable to the comparison of the present multiple-site study with a previous single-site investigation. Alternatively, given the extensive time lapse between the studies, changes in experience and opinion between differing generations of students may also have influenced the reported findings. More recently, Gordon and Grant (1997) have reported some adverse evaluation of teachers by young adolescents but unfortunately offered no data to indicate the proportion of their sample involved.

Problems with Sex or Drugs

Relatively few adolescents in this sample identified sex (17%) or drugs (15%) as personal problems for which they would be likely to likely to require help. These data support the opinion of Falchikov (1986), who concluded that issues of sex and drugs identified with adolescence by the mass media are out of proportion to the actual extent of adolescent preoccupations. In contrast to the findings of Violato and Holden (1988) for Canadian adolescents, no significant age effects were found for drug-related problems, and the same was true for concerns about sex; however, cultural variables may have contributed to this difference in findings.

Problems with Mental Health

Only 13 percent of the sample identified their mind and just 11 percent mentioned their dreams as likely topics for help. Such findings suggest that among these secondary students, there was a general absence of concern about their mental health at either conscious or unconscious levels of functioning. This data supports the notion of adolescence as a normal period of human development. It also lends some support to those professionals who view adolescence as a period with a relatively low incidence of mental health problems (see, for example, the work of Offord et al. 1987).

Problems with Religion

Only 6 percent of the respondents indicated that religion was a problem that they would be likely to require help with. In relation to this finding, it may be relevant that Phelps and Jarvis (1994) noted that the religion subscale of their coping inventory did not load on any factor included in their study. This lead them to suggest that religious views are not well defined in adolescence. However, there are two other possible interpretations to consider in the context of this survey. First, there is the possibility that adolescent involvement in religion is common, but that it poses few personal problems. Second, there is the alternative view that this type of problem is uncommon because adolescents have little involvement in religion.

It is difficult to make a judgment within the bounds of this survey, which did not set out to resolve such questions. Fortunately, other surveys of English adolescents provide some assistance. Reid (1977, 1980) has reported that only 6 percent of teenagers attended church weekly and just 4 percent monthly. Nonetheless, Homan and Youngman (1982) found that the religious knowledge of secondary school students was enhanced by attending Sunday School. However, Reid's data also showed that 40 percent of twelve to fifteen year olds had never attended Sunday School, and only 3 percent still attended at the point when their opinions were sought. Regarding the infrequent reporting of religious problems in the present survey, the hypothesis that adolescents have little involvement with organized religion therefore appears to offer the more probable interpretation. We should note in passing that the survey data do not indicate that adolescence lacks some element of spiritual aspiration.

Summary of Key Findings on Personal Problems

Despite a strong indication by over half of the students that they had already solved some problems for themselves, this investigation identifies a core of basic adolescent concerns (regarding issues of career, relationships, schoolwork, and the self) which shows considerable consistency between cultures and across the last two decades. Nonetheless, outside of the core concerns, evidence of some significant new issues appears to have emerged quite recently. (Furthermore, the problems identified in this investigation were accompanied by a widespread adolescent perception that they would probably need some form of help with them.) These findings also differ qualitatively from previous research, which has restricted itself mainly to identifying adolescent problems. In the present study, registering the presence of a problem formed only a part of the requirement. An additional necessity was that the problems identified were those which students were most likely to require help with, that is, problems for which they would probably need to augment with their own coping resources in order to solve them.

There were no significant differences between year groups in the frequency of reporting any of the problems listed; however, there were variations between the sexes. Significantly more males identified their career as a personal problem ($p < 0.01$) while significantly more females ($p < 0.001$) cited their feelings, their looks, their body, their relationships, sex, and schoolwork ($p < 0.01$) as problems. A predominance of females reporting emotional or physical concerns has also been recently reported by Caspar, Belanoff, and Offer (1996); Dubow et al. (1990); Gordon and Grant (1997); and Rhode and Bellfield (1992).

The finding of differential responding between the sexes but not across year groups is seemingly at variance with the work of Stark et al. (1989), who found significant differences on both variables. However, this divergence may be explicable in terms of the inclusion of seventeen-year-olds, the use of Likert-type ratings, and cultural differences in the Stark et al. study. Nonetheless, these workers also noted that differences on the sex variable were more pronounced in their study than were differences between younger and older adolescents.

Adolescent Coping

One-third or more of the present sample (between 34% and 80% according to the problem specified) regarded it as unlikely that they would need help with any problem category listed. This result is broadly consistent with the research of Walker, Harris, Blum, Schneider, and Resnick (1990), in which 84 percent of a large adolescent sample stated that they did not have problems for which they had needed help during the previous year. The present finding is taken to imply that either many students did not have the relevant problems at the time of the survey, or that if they did, they could manage them without recourse to help from others. Given that approximately 90 percent of the students identified one or more personal problems, the second implication appears more probable.

Moreover, an overall 71 percent of the students reported solving some or a lot of problems without help from anyone else. Further analysis of problem-solving reports showed that significantly more students in the later year groups (p < 0.01) reported that they had solved some problems without help from anyone else. Similarly, the number of respondents indicating that they had solved no problems decreased (p < 0.01) across later year groups. These findings suggest a lasting adolescent commitment to management of their own problems and the possibility of an association between progress through school and increasing self-reliance.

Results of this survey also indicate that both rational and emotional types of coping were reported. The most common overall pattern was initial worrying (38%) and later independent problem solving (53%). The next most likely reaction was that students initially told themselves that the situation could be worse (21%) and later asked someone else to help solve the problem (31%). Involvement of others when trying to handle negative feelings was also reported by 38 percent of Gordon and Grant's (1997) sample. The least common response was initially crying (3%) and later asking someone to solve the problem for them (2%). Infrequent recourse to tears in these English adolescents is paralleled by a similar low frequency of reported crying (below 5%) in Gordon and Grant's Scottish secondary school students.

Rational Coping

Rational coping activity was reported by both sexes. Males more frequently indicated (p < 0.001) that they employed the tactics of thinking about something else; of telling themselves that things could be worse; and of trying to solve the problem themselves. Coping by means of diverting attention was also reported by Brown et al. (1986). Some caution should be exercised in comparing the two studies, however, since the precise meaning of the term "attention diversion" used by these authors was not defined.

Over twice as many male students as females reported that they did nothing in the face of personal problems (p < 0.001). This result is notionally in keeping with the findings of Phelps and Jarvis (1994), who reported that males employ more avoidant coping strategies than females. In the present research, however, only 8 percent of the total sample recorded avoidant coping techniques, so that the statistical difference is actually based upon a very small proportion of the respondents. Since the Phelps and Jarvis study did not include percentage data, it is not clear what proportion of their sample provided the data to support that conclusion. Accordingly, it is inferred that the present research provides no more than weak support for the avoidant male-coping hypothesis. This interpretation is reinforced by the work of Copeland and Hess (1995), who found that avoiding problems was ranked eleven out of thirteen coping patterns for both males and females in their study.

Females more commonly indicated (p<.001) that they reacted by worrying (one-third more females than males); or by asking someone else to help them to solve the problem. These findings are in keeping with research from other cultures (Bird & Harris 1990; Patterson & McGubbin 1987; Rickwood 1992; Ryan, Stiller, & Lynch 1994; Sieffge-Krenke 1990). However, it remains possible that both independent problem solving and shared problem solving represent different types of adolescent coping behavior.

Emotional Coping

The more intensely emotive reactions such as getting angry or crying were particularly uncommon, being recorded by only 10 percent and 3 percent of the sample. The distribution of emotional reactions differed (p < 0.001), however. First, significantly more males than females reported reacting to problems with anger, a finding which is supported by the work of Bird and Harris (1990) and Greene (1988). Second, sixteen times more females than males recorded crying when they had a personal problem. Differential female recourse to crying has also been reported by Copeland and Hess (1995) and Gordon and Grant (1997).

In addition, more males than females (p < 0.001) indicated that they released emotional tension by laughing about their problems. Patterson and McGubbin (1987) also found that adolescent males had a higher mean score than females on the use of humor as a coping response, although it was not apparent what proportion of their sample was involved. Phelps and Jarvis (1994) have reported that both sexes use humor relatively infrequently when dealing with problems. In contrast, Copeland and Hess (1995) found that being humorous was included in the top four coping strategies reported by both males and females, so that outcomes differ between the few studies available. However, as no more than 4 percent of secondary students from the present study indicated laughing at their problems, current data support the proposition that humor may be used relatively little by adolescents when coping with personal problems.

The data from part one of the survey encourage the view that these early to midadolescents had developed a considerable degree of self-reliance, although they had not done so at the price of sacrificing their relationships within or between generations. It therefore appears possible that their relationships with friends and family members may be associated with a tendency to use a relatively controlled approach to solving personal problems. Moreover, the common problem-solving strategies reported for adolescents by Sieffge-Krenke (1990), which included active problem resolution, cognitive redefinition, and reducing emotional tension, were also employed by the English teenagers who participated in this study.

Summary of the Findings on Adolescent Coping

The data discussed indicate that independent attempts to cope with personal problems are common during early to midadolescence. In contrast, reported behaviors implying dependency or avoidance appear to be uncommon. Moreover, these are important findings for potential helpers. If adolescents already have a repertoire of coping skills, then those who seek help from others may bring with them personal resources which could potentially be used to attenuate the impact of their problems. Therefore the task of helping should arguably include efforts to access information about existing adolescent coping strategies in order to create more meaningful solutions.

DISCUSSION OF THE PART TWO FINDINGS ON SCHOOL INFORMATION

STUDENT PROFILE TWO

A representative secondary school student knows that it is possible to get help for personal problems in their school. If he or she decides to approach a member of staff for help, it will probably be his or her form teacher. The head or deputy headteacher are the least likely persons to be approached. Access to the form tutor is believed to be easy, and if this route is taken, then the student would expect to wait only minutes to get the help required. However, in the past he or she has most likely neither wanted nor asked for teacher assistance with a personal problem and therefore has not yet received such help in school.

Awareness of Help

Fisher (1983) points out that research on help giving reflects a dominant social belief that helping others is a good thing which should be encouraged. In accordance with this view it would therefore seem reasonable to expect that some provision for helping others should be readily apparent within our schools. Since the majority of adolescents in this sample (53%) reported that help for personal problems was available to them in their own school, it appears that an established facility for student support had achieved widespread recognition. However, with the remaining 47 percent of students apparently believing that help was not available to them or being unaware of its existence, the level of student awareness was far from being comprehensive.

It did not prove possible to locate a body of literature that had specifically addressed student knowledge of facilities for getting help with personal problems in school. Accordingly, it is concluded that the data in the preceding paragraph provide new information on adolescent awareness of school-based helping.

Choice of Helper

When identifying potential helpers in school, more students (25% of the sample) selected their form tutor than any other member of the teaching staff. This proportion differs markedly from that reported in the one other study found to include a form tutor option. Murgatroyd (1977) reported that 9 percent of his sample chose their form teacher as a potential helper. Murgatroyd's key question was posed in this way: "If you felt the need to talk to someone about a problem—someone in school, a friend, or parent, or anyone, who would you talk to" (Murgatroyd 1977: 75)? Three categories of problem were then specified. These included a personal–private problem, a career problem, and a problem connected with school.

The present study linked two questions, with the second one providing the item under consideration. The first of these (item 2.1 on the questionnaire) asked, "Is it possible to get help with a personal problem in your school?" The second question (labelled as item 2.2) asked, "Who would you go to for this kind of help in school?" Five different teacher options were included with separate boxes for the students to check. Hence the two studies employed somewhat different methodology. The 16 percent difference in nominating form teachers between studies may therefore be accounted for by procedural variations, changes in schools and students during the intervening years, and the contrast between a single-site and a multiple-site investigation.

Two-thirds more students in the present sample chose their form tutor than their head of year. In addition, the form tutors were selected four times more often than subject teachers, twelve times more often than deputy headteachers, and twenty-five times more often than headteachers. These ratios portray a reduced scale of student endorsement for more senior staff as helpers. This finding suggests that formality and infrequent contact may reduce student perceptions of helping potential in others. The small number of students (5%) indicating that they would approach a school doctor for help lends some credence to this notion.

These data provide a range of information about adolescent choice of helper in schools that was previously unavailable. (Earlier studies of adolescent help seeking have for the most part failed to distinguish adequately between the differing types of teaching staff.) Such information is important because secondary schools are complex organizations employing large numbers of teachers from whom potential helpers may be chosen.

Use of Support in School

Virtually two-thirds of the students (65%) reported that access to their helper was easy or very easy, suggesting some association between availability and choice of helper. Ease of access was probably an important consideration in the context of adolescent expectations for waiting time. Two items of information underline the relevance of this point. First, more than half of the adolescent respondents (52%) expected to wait only minutes or hours for help, and for two-thirds of this group, minutes was the chosen response. Second, only a small number (15%) expected to wait days or weeks, so that immediacy of support was the general expectation. For the minority of students who had asked a teacher to talk over one of their problems, results suggested that most of them got a rapid response. Only 16 percent reported waiting days or weeks for teacher help. These figures reiterate the importance of a finding by Adelman (1993) that ease of access is one of the important determinants in the use of school-based support during adolescence.

Data that indicated the extent to which adolescents orientate toward the supportive resources of their school were equally striking. Here, 78 percent recorded that they had rarely or never wanted a teacher to talk over one of their problems with them, backed by 89 percent reporting that they had rarely or never asked for this to happen. This suggests a considerable overlap between reported student attitudes and reported behaviors. Moreover, when asked if they had actually received help with a personal problem in school, 18 percent responded that they had while 82 percent indicated that they had not. This finding provides support for the work of Wintre et al. (1988), who reported a low level of adolescent support from adult experts for problem-solving purposes.

Summary of Key Findings on Main Variables

A key finding is here defined as one involving 51 percent or more of the sample. Findings involving a minority of the sample are not discussed because in many cases they involve such small numbers of students and therefore may lack widespread psychological or practical significance.

Key Findings by Sex

Only one of the recorded differences on the sex variable derived from a questionnaire item on which more than 50 percent of the sample responded. Significantly more females than males (p < 0.001) indicated that it was possible to get help with a personal problem in school (this finding was based upon 53% of the sample responding). Since it was found in part one of the questionnaire that females reported having more personal problems, this elevated level of awareness may be related to greater support-seeking experience in school.

Key Findings by Year Group

The absence of year group differences suggests a variety of possibilities. First, it might indicate that basic information about how their student support system operates is widely disseminated by teachers. Second, it seems possible that this body of information might be assimilated by students early in the secondary phase of their education and retained thereafter. Third, it may be that the relevant knowledge base, either as presented or as later modified by the students themselves, serves their decision making adequately across years eight through ten. A fourth possibility is that as far as adolescents are concerned, the delivered knowledge base may be largely irrelevant to their management of personal problems in school. Further investigation would be required to resolve these issues satisfactorily.

Key Findings by School

For this part of the questionnaire, there was only one significant difference on the school variable which involved the majority of the sample. Significantly more students from school six ($p < 0.0005$) indicated that help was available in school, a finding which was based upon 53 percent of the sample responding on this item. School six was the only one that had an open door policy regarding parent contact and that had trained parent volunteers to assist students with learning difficulties. It may therefore be that these arrangements influenced adolescent opinion of the school's helping resources. With that single exception, however, the findings highlight how infrequently substantive differences occurred on the school variable.

Key Findings by Location

There were no significant differences in the location data; therefore, between urban and rural students, the outstanding attribute of findings on the location variable is consistency.

DISCUSSION OF THE PART THREE FINDINGS ON STUDENT HELP PREFERENCES

STUDENT PROFILE THREE

A representative secondary school student prefers a friend of the same age and same sex as their helper. If the student has to choose a teacher, however, he or she will probably choose their form tutor. In deciding how to make the first contact with the form tutor, the student is likely to opt for a direct approach on their own behalf, rather than getting someone else to speak for them. Their preferred mode of meeting would be a face-to-face interaction taking place in a school office on a one-to-one basis. The single favorite time for such a meeting would be after school has finished.

In the course of the meeting, the student would like to be asked what was the matter and encouraged to talk about the current problem. He or she would also like to be asked about his or her feelings. The preferred helper intervention would be to suggest optional ways of handling the problem and to offer potential solutions. Contact with the helper is most likely to be terminated if they tell others what the student had said. Nonetheless, in framing advice for a friend on how to cope with a personal problem, the student would first suggest that in seeking help they should also ask a friend.

Preferred Helper Attributes

In this sample of secondary students the preference for friends or parents as helpers far exceeds the level of support given to any other group referred to. A favorable perception of friends and parents as helpers has previously been reported by Hortacsu (1989). Furman and Buhrmester (1985) also showed that as helpers, friends and parents received the highest ratings from young people. With more than twice as many students choosing friends as opted for their own parents (57% to 25%) in the present study, adolescent preferences operated strongly in favor of friends as helpers. This finding supports that of Rhode and Bellfield (1992) who also reported a ratio of approximately 2:1 adolescents favoring friends over parents as helpers. Although adolescents sometimes establish an alliance with the parents of a friend, this option was not popular regarding help for a personal problem, being selected by only 5 percent of the sample. Friendship appears to be particularly important, in that barely 1 percent indicated a preference for another student as a helper, suggesting that peer-group membership in itself may not confer helper status.

These findings extend and support the conclusion of Adelman (1993) that help is sought more from friends than from family members. They also reinforce the views of Hunter and Youniss (1982) and Kandel and Lesser (1969a) that adolescents are more likely to utilize friends than parents when coping with problems. Moreover, they are consistent with the opinion of Paterson, Field, and Pryor (1994) that friends are consulted more regarding existential problems. Rosenburg (1965) found that parental advice was, however, sought more than that of peers when there were important decisions to be made. Adolescent support seeking from parents has also been confirmed by the work of Berndt and Miller (1989); Hendry, Roberts, and Glendinning (1992); Keys and Fernandes (1992); Porteous and Fisher (1980); Siann, Draper, and Cosford (1982); and Whitney and Smith (1992).

Consequently both friends and parents appear to be regarded as important helpers during adolescence, although the evidence for a long-term trend is mixed. Some researchers suggest that as adolescents get older, they seek support from parents less and friends more (Boldero & Fallon 1995; Hunter & Youniss 1982; Papini et al. 1990; Wintre et al. 1988). Others suggest that support-seeking remains fairly constant through the adolescent years for both parents and friends (Greenberg, Seigel, and Leitch 1993; Hill 1993; Ryan, Stiller, & Lynch 1994). Such issues are settled for this sample by the finding that that the preference for parents as helpers declined by 44 percent across year groups (p < 0.02).

There was no significant change across year groups in preferring friends as helpers, but there was a nonsignificant trend indicating an increasing number of students in later year groups who nominated friends. (The relevant totals were 75 in year eight; 87 in year nine; and 91 in year ten, yielding an overall increase of 21%.) These data lend qualified support to the view that more adolescents prefer friends as helpers by midadolescence, and less prefer parents, at least as far as support for personal problems is concerned.

Further adolescent stipulation favored a same-sex helper (57%) of the same age (47%) replicating the findings of three earlier studies (Adams & Adams 1991; Northman 1978; Wintre et al. 1988). Only 12 percent of the sample preferred an opposite-sex helper. An older helper came in as a close second preference (43%). There was most support among this subgroup, however, for someone just a little older (27%), with only 16 percent favoring someone a lot older. Northman (1978) reported similar support for someone a little older in an American student sample. In the present study, younger helpers were not a popular choice, since they were the stated preference of a mere 1 percent of the students.

Shell and Eisenberg (1992) have advanced an interesting explanation for the preference of an older helper over a younger helper. They surmise that since older siblings often take up the role of helper in the family, children may become conditioned early on in their lives to expect help from older persons, or to feel humiliated by help from a younger person. In learning contexts, these workers believe that older helpers may be preferred because of situational role expectations.

Adolescents may also discriminate between helpers in terms of the assistance that they can offer for different types of problem. For example, Meeus (1989) found that young people in Holland felt more supported by mothers regarding peer group problems, while Wintre et al. (1988) noted that Canadian adolescents preferred peer advice in the face of serious conflict between their parents. Boldero and Fallon (1995) concluded that Australian adolescents tended to seek help from a friend regarding interpersonal problems, a teacher for educational problems, and another professional for health problems, results which were in keeping with those of Evans and Poole (1987) and Frydenberg and Lewis (1993).

A preference for help from a teacher rather than a peer, a parent, or another professional accounted for less than 2 percent of the student responses, well below the 13 percent of teacher nominations obtained by Armacost (1990). This outcome is in accord with Galbo's (1994) view that teachers are seldom found to be personally significant for a large percentage of adolescents, given students' established utilization of friends and parents for personal support. Given that Furman and Buhrmester (1985) noted that teachers were turned to mostly for instrumental aid, and Nelson-Le Gall and Gummerman (1984) found that young people preferred teacher help for academically focused problems, perhaps it is to be expected that their assistance is only weakly supported for problems of a personal nature. Rickwood (1992) has also observed that adolescents demonstrate a preference for nonprofessional helpers. Teachers may take some comfort from the finding in the present study that secondary school students also gave minimal support to the helper options of either another professional or another student.

Helper Contact Preferences

It is of some interest that when considering getting help from a teacher, three-quarters of the sample said that they would prefer to make contact for themselves. This option was supported ten times more frequently than referral by a friend, fifteen times more often than referral via their family, and seventy-five times more often than referral by another teacher. In addition, the desire for personal contact as the initial mode of interaction far outstripped contact by letter or contact by telephone, being chosen at least fifteen times more frequently.

Most adolescents wanted a face-to-face meeting (71%) in a one-to-one context (52%). Meeting with a teacher in the company of another person was a less well-supported alternative. While just under one-third of the sample (31%) wished to meet with a friend present, only 3 percent wanted to meet in a group of other students with problems; only 6 percent wanted a parent to be there; and just 2 percent wished their whole family to be present. These findings support the opinion of Karabenick and Knapp (1991) that help seeking in an academic context may be related more to student competency than to dependency. Moreover, they serve as a caution to those professionals who automatically choose to intervene with group or family-focused interventions.

To conclude this section, a preference for daytime meetings, either in or out of school time, were favored by three-quarters of the students. The most popular single time was after school, with just 5 percent preferring an evening meeting. Only 15 percent wanted, however, to meet a helper during lessons, so there was little evidence that the majority of the students saw meeting a teacher as an excuse to get out of their classes. An ideal location appeared to be a school office, with over twice as many students choosing this alternative over any other school location, and four times more did so than expressed a wish to meet at home. The general desire to meet alone and in an office might imply that students do not wish to be observed or overheard, an implication which is strengthened by the finding that less than 3 percent wanted to make contact with a helper in a corridor or the school library.

Helper Communication Preferences

A particularly important aspect of the students' opinion was the emphasis that they placed upon wanting helpers to adopt an active role throughout the helping interaction. When asked a range of questions about what they would like to happen if they needed help, direct helper assistance was repeatedly endorsed. One-third or more of the students wanted to be asked what was the matter and to talk about their problem, suggesting that problem-related conversation was considered necessary. Almost one-half of the respondents wanted to be asked how they felt, and just under a third wanted to be asked questions about their feelings. Hence talking about both their problems and their feelings appeared important for a substantial proportion of the sample.

By far the most frequently indicated adolescent disposition, however, was that of wanting helpers to give them suggestions. This preference took two forms. First, there was a widespread need for helpers to suggest alternative ways of working out student problems (62%). Second, an even larger majority wanted helpers to suggest possible solutions for their problems (69%). These findings indicate that one reason for adolescents to seek support in school is that they may not always have ready-made solutions themselves. Moreover, it is possible they find that coping with a particular personal problem calls for skills or resources that they do not initially possess. Therefore, although there are differing forms of assistance that are in keeping with student preferences, solution-focused interventions seem to feature strongly among the favored alternatives.

These communication preferences complement traditional models of the helping process in several respects, for example, in talking about problems and feelings. They also call into question, however, certain aspects of conventional practice in the context of helping adolescents. The majority preference for helper suggestions is one which challenges the validity of an entirely nondirective model of helping for secondary school students. Similarly, only one student in ten wanted a helper to summarize their problem, so that paraphrasing did not appear to be a major student priority. Since there was negligible support for helpers waiting for students to speak first, there is also evidence that the clinical practice of inducing deliberate silences may be unproductive in school-based helping. Moreover, where these techniques inhibit helpers from offering constructive suggestions to young people seeking assistance, a genuine concern arises regarding the basic assumptions being made. Findings from this research suggest that they may not be founded upon views of adolescents themselves and consequently may not adequately represent a professional ideal of client-centered helping.

Termination Issues

Another significant feature of the research reported is that it underlines how highly students regard the issue of privacy in the context of their school community. One of the primary reasons that 47 percent of these teenagers gave for making a decision to terminate contact with a helper was that of the provider disclosing personal information. This perspective received significantly more support from students in year ten ($p < 0.001$). The level of response on this issue is much higher than the 13 percent showing concern over possible violations of their confidence reported by Kayser-Boyd, Adelman, and Taylor (1985). The magnitude of this difference may derive from variations in adolescent experience and environmental or cultural factors over time and between the American and English research sites involved. The identification of concern about disclosure in the present sample is nonetheless in accord with the assertion of McGuire et al. (1994) that children value privacy in helping relationships and are negatively affected by threats of unauthorized disclosure.

It is of interest that U.K. data supporting this proposition have been furnished by the Greater Glasgow Health Board (Gordon & Grant 1997). This research indicates that the reluctance of young secondary school students to consult teachers was founded partly upon fears that the nature of their consultation would be disclosed to parents. The importance attributed to privacy by these adolescents is underlined by the second reason given for deciding to terminate contact, namely that of being asked questions that were too personal, which suggests that it may be essential to explore adolescent views about the range of the helping agenda before it is implemented.

Indeed, Gelso and Carter (1994) view the strength of the working alliance as being affected by the extent to which the helper and client agree on the goals of their work and upon the tasks that are useful to attain the goals agreed. Closer attention to these issues may be productive in assisting young people to maintain helping relationships. It also seems desirable on the ground that early termination seems common, given O'Leary's (1979) finding that 45 percent of young people discontinued counselor contact as early as session two of a potentially longer series.

Advice to Friends

The most commonly indicated recommendation to a friend with a personal problem was to ask a friend (30%), closely followed by that of asking a parent (28%). These options were exercised almost twice as often as that of asking a teacher. The only other located study to pose the question of what advice would be given to friends (Wiggins & Moody 1987) did not include an option for choosing significant others or teachers, since it focused on counselors. Going by the results already discussed, one explanation as to why remote helping facilities (such as Childline and magazine advice columns) received very few endorsements may therefore be found in the strong adolescent preference for getting assistance from trusted individuals who already feature as significant others.

The publicity generated to promote the national Childline may have been picked up by this sample of students, but only 8 percent indicated that this would be the direction in which they would point their friends, reiterating the low adolescent priority assigned to telephone contact. Similarly, despite the widespread targeting of teenagers by magazine publishers in recent years, a mere 3 percent of the sample stated that they would suggest the pursuit of that option to friends having problems. It seems probable that both the Childline and magazine alternatives may to some extent be handicapped by limited familiarity. Delay in obtaining assistance (a valid consideration in trying to contact a busy telephone number or awaiting a response from a magazine advice column) may also be of significance, since findings from part two of the questionnaire indicated that these students generally anticipated waiting only a few minutes for help.

Summary of Key Findings on Main Variables

Key Findings by Sex

Of the significant (p < 0.001) sex differences reported in Chapter 4, greatest weight is assigned to the four items that involved a majority (i.e., more than 51%) of the total number of students responding. These were preferring to meet a helper alone, having a helper of the same sex, getting help from a friend, and having the helper give suggestions. Male predominance was found on one of these items, and female predominance on three others. Two-thirds more males than females indicated that they would prefer to meet a helper alone (based upon 52% of the sample). However, one-fifth more females than males preferred a friend as a helper, and four-fifths favored a helper of the same sex (57% of the sample responding in each case). Approximately 25 percent more females than males wanted the helper to give them suggestions (based on 62% of the sample responding). These findings suggest that in seeking help for personal problems, more males tend to uphold their independence, while more females than males regard the quality of interpersonal contact as being important.

Key Findings by Year Group

On the year group variable, only two of the significant findings reported were derived from items for which more than 50 percent of the sample had responded. Here, significantly more year ten students (p < 0.01) preferred to meet a helper alone (a finding based on 52% of the sample). Also, more year ten students (p < 0.01) wanted a helper to suggest a possible solution for their problem (62% of the sample responding on this item). These data suggest that privacy becomes a particularly salient issue for more senior students. Given the evidence discussed earlier (that there is no significant increase in the number of personal problems reported), an alternative explanation may be that students' need for suggested solutions is related to an increasing complexity of problems from year eight through year ten.

Key Findings by School or Location

In the results for part three there were no reported findings on the school or location which were derived from a majority of the sample, so that overall consistency is the central characteristic of the findings for these variables.

DISCUSSION OF THE PART FOUR FINDINGS ON STUDENT EXPERIENCE OF TEACHER SUPPORT

STUDENT PROFILE FOUR

A representative secondary school student sought teacher help of his or her own volition. He or she was looked at by the teacher, asked to talk about the problem, and required to talk about personal feelings. The teacher involved said that he or she would help, offered alternatives for dealing with the problem, and suggested some possible solutions. Most of the assistance given was in keeping with what the student expected and was regarded as helpful. Subsequently the problem got better and sometimes went away completely. In certain instances, the help also assisted with additional problems that were not specifically addressed, most often with a problem that was old. In other cases, no effect on the student's other problems was recorded. While communicating with a helper, the student found it particularly easy to talk about bullying, their feelings, and schoolwork.

The paucity of research on adolescent help seeking alluded to by Ostrov (1985) is nowhere more apparent than in the context of their views of helping interventions. By examining adolescent experience of school-based helping, this part of the survey provides information on the acceptability of specific procedures and helper behaviors. Moreover, it does so in a context where the respondents had received teacher support for personally meaningful problems.

Rationale for Seeking Support

Self-referrals ran at almost double the number of referrals that were made at the recommendation of either a friend or a parent and more than ten times the proportion made at the recommendation of a teacher. These findings suggest strong student commitment toward being proactive in searching for solutions. They also help to sustain the view that support seeking can be construed as a sign of adolescent coping rather than one of dependency upon others. In addition, the above ratio of referrals indicates that the influence of friends and parents in deciding to seek support is much more frequently recorded than that of teachers.

Experience of Teacher Rapport

A substantial proportion of these adolescents reported empathic behaviors on the part of the teachers with whom they had discussed personal problems. These behaviors included looking at the students (44%); greeting them (29%); and using their first names (34%). These actions were backed up by asking the students how they felt (47%); inquiring if they had told anyone else about their feelings (40%); asking related questions (71%); and appearing interested (34%). The teachers also built rapport by nodding their heads (31%); telling students not to worry (56%); saying they would help (54%); or telling them about a similar problem of their own (21%). A further 9 percent of the students indicated that their teachers had said something nice about them.

Student reports therefore suggest that they most commonly experienced teachers engaging in exploratory questions or providing reassurance. According to this sample, teachers used questions more than three times as often as self-disclosure and seven times more often than compliments. Accordingly, it may be that certain aspects of developing rapport deserve greater emphasis in relation to helping troubled adolescents. For example, Mills (1985) found that many adolescents found it difficult to start talking, although they revealed more information later on when self-disclosure had been modeled by their helper.

Experience of the Helping Intervention

It appears from the information provided by the students that teachers adopted a problem-solving orientation. Approximately one-half of the students indicated that they were asked to talk about their problem and were asked questions about it. Only 13 percent recorded that teachers had gone on to describe their problem in a few words, but 46 percent noted that their teachers had suggested alternatives for handling the problem. Contrary to the early traditions of the counseling movement, it appears that teachers employed paraphrasing of problems infrequently and were willing to provide problem-related advice.

According to the data however, attempts to harness the personal resources of the students for problem-solving purposes was relatively uncommon. Less than one-quarter of the sample reported that they had been asked for their ideas, or questioned how they had solved other problems, or if they knew a possible solution for the problem at hand. Yet almost 60 percent indicated that teachers had suggested a possible solution. This appears to be a constructive practice, insofar as Engen, Laing, and Sawyer (1988) reported that 39 percent of their adolescents believed problem solving to be one of the main benefits of getting help. Teachers referred to in the current study were often perceived as demonstrating appropriate interpersonal skills and sometimes as using particular counseling techniques such as nonverbal cueing, exploratory questioning, or self-disclosure. In contrast, however, the use of ego-building statements and drawing upon the student's own repertoire of coping skills was rarely reported.

It might therefore be concluded that teacher intervention appears to have been built upon both cognitive and affective components, which are broadly in accord with the range of experiences that students indicated they would prefer to encounter in school-based helping situations. In addition, the reported range of teacher behaviors seems compatible with a student preference for contact with teachers who are friendly, listen, stay calm, and deal fairly with problems (Branwhite 1988) and with teachers who exhibit qualities like those of their friends, such as honesty, trust, and a caring approach (Galbo 1994). Moreover, the evidence from this study points to teachers providing active intervention, an approach which is in keeping with the assertion of Garmezy and Rutter (1985) that just talking through problems may be an invalid form of support for children. However, it also appears that there is considerable scope for making more use of adolescents' personal resourcefulness.

Student Expectation and Evaluation of Help Received

Far from being reluctant to attribute any benefit to the helping encounter, two-thirds of those who sought support from their teachers indicated that most or all of their expectations had been met. Moreover, 59 percent of those who had received teacher assistance evaluated it as quite helpful or very helpful. This compares favorably with satisfaction levels recorded in other school-based studies of secondary level students. Satisfaction with school counselors, for example, ranges from 24 percent (Newport 1977) to 59 percent (Engen, Laing, and Sawyer 1988).

The present research also measures up well to satisfaction levels of 57 percent for listening or 37 percent for advice from peer counselors (Morey et al. 1989); and 40 percent for intervention from a psychiatric service family therapy team (Dunne & Thompson 1995). It is not as high, however, as the 90 percent level reported for seventeen to eighteen year olds in a Los Angeles high school (Adelman 1993), a difference which may be accounted for by divergence in age, school, and cultural variables between the two samples involved. In the current study, not only were the students in early to midadolescence, but they were from a variety of urban and rural English schools. The absence of any significant difference in satisfaction levels between the sexes recorded in this study reinforces a finding by Northman (1985).

Effects of the Intervention

Notwithstanding positive adolescent perceptions of help received, the question remains of how far the students believed that they derived any benefit from intervention provided. On this separate but equally important issue, a majority of the recipients of teacher assistance again provided a positive response. Two-thirds of this student sample reported that they obtained either a reduction or a cessation of the referred problem, while a further 9 percent gained a temporary respite. This not only attests to a general adolescent perception of the effectiveness of teacher intervention, but it compares favorably with a recent 50 percent adolescent endorsement of benefit derived from treatment received in an adolescent psychiatric unit (Stuart-Smith 1994). Moreover, 38 percent of the students in the present study recorded that their problem had got better but did not go away, and this contrasts favorably with the 85 percent of an adolescent unit sample reporting that their problems had continued in some form (Wells et al. 1978).

In relation to the issue of whether the help provided was generalized by the recipients to other problems, no one-way outcome was derived. Indeed, the data were evenly divided, with close to one-third of the students who had received teacher assistance with their personal problem saying that it had also helped them with other problems, and virtually the same proportion indicating that it had not helped with other problems. One possible explanation for this finding is that the helping approach yielded a ripple effect for other problems, when the teachers concerned had employed a general-case problem-solving strategy, but that it yielded no such benefit when only problem-specific guidance was given.

Identification of Easy and Difficult Topics

The present investigation extends an earlier line of inquiry to a wider range of issues. Only one previous study was found to report adolescent opinion on the value of topics discussed with a school-based helper. Mills (1985) reported that hobbies and relationships with others were popular, but unhappy times were perceived as the most difficult topic to talk about. However, two constraints of this approach are that hobbies generally seem unlikely to be a source of personal problems, and unhappy times constitute a broad category that may conceal a range of more specific issues.

In the current study, hobbies were not included for the reason already given, and relationships were classed as easy to talk about by only 15 percent of the respondents. The topic most often classed as easy for this sample was bullying (47%). Feelings were the topic most frequently categorized as hard to talk about (32%). However, opinions on other topics ranged between these two extremes. Differences in findings between these two studies can probably be accounted for by variations in sample size (50 in the earlier study and 540 in the current study); in the gender distribution (three times more males than females in the prior investigation, and equal numbers here); in culture (Canadian versus English adolescents); and in research technique (interview versus survey).

With reference to the ease or difficulty of communication across the range of topics covered, bullying, feelings, and schoolwork were rated easy by 34 to 47 percent of the respondents. Just one topic (feelings) received a comparable level of citation (32%) as being hard to talk about. Support for the idea that personal feelings can be both an "easy" and a "hard" domain to talk about is a somewhat paradoxical finding. In fact, 42 percent of the students who had received help from a teacher reported that their feelings had been easy to talk about, 32 percent indicated that feelings had been hard to discuss, and just under 2 percent that their feelings had been both easy and hard to talk about. Hence it appears that students classifying feelings as either easy or hard to talk about is probably represented by different subsets of the range of individuals involved.

Three possible explanations for differing student perceptions about discussing their feelings arise. First, these findings might imply the existence of individual differences in adolescent perception, that is, that certain individuals normally find feelings easy to talk about, while others usually find it hard to do so. Second, during the adolescent years students may find that each perception holds true at times (e.g., that attributes like the quality, intensity, or variation in feelings may sometimes be easy and sometimes be difficult to communicate to a helper). Third, these possibilities are not mutually exclusive and therefore may interact at times. Out of the three topics retrospectively classed as "easy," two of them (feelings and schoolwork) had been identified by 33 percent or more of the students in part one of the survey as problems for which students would be likely to need help.

Summary of Key Findings on Main Variables

Key Findings by Sex

Although the survey findings included significant differences on the sex and year group variables, none of those reported in the results were based upon a majority of the students responding to the items involved.

Key Findings by Year Group

Since no significant differences occurred on the year group variable in part four of the questionnaire, there are no majority findings to discuss.

Key Findings by School

Two items yielded significant differences ($p < 0.001$) involving a majority of the sample. School six produced the most students of any school who reported that it was possible to get help for personal problems in school (a finding based upon the 53% of the sample who responded to this item). School five had the most students who indicated that they had never asked for help (with 72% of the sample responding). Findings on the school variable were therefore characterized by widespread agreement.

Key Findings by Location

Since no significant differences occurred on the location variable in part four of the questionnaire, it follows that no majority findings are available for discussion. The level of agreement between urban and rural students is therefore very high.

Overview of Key Findings on Main Variables

The overall pattern of findings on the four main variables analyzed for each part of the questionnaire is that significant differences involving a majority of the sample accounted for just a very small proportion of the findings. This view is reinforced by a complete absence of significant differences on the year group and location variables in part two and part four of the questionnaire. An outstanding feature of the survey data accordingly appears to be one of extensive agreement between the participating students.

6

Implications for
School Development

Helping clients construct the future is a critical helper man-
date.

Egan 1990, 274

This study has established that multiple problems and a clear pattern of support needs to exist among secondary school students.
However, the identification of student problems and needs cannot
in itself constitute an adequate school-level response. Investigation can only highlight the ecology of the educational world of adolescence. It follows, however, that concerned professionals can
recognize the need to transform new knowledge into appropriate
action that will impact directly upon identified student needs. Accordingly, this chapter will consider some of the professional issues involved in creating the kind of progress required in the pursuit
of excellent student support services.

THE HELPING POTENTIAL OF ADOLESCENTS

It has long been recognized that adolescence is a time of evolving
cognitive and social dynamics, but more recently Magen and
Aharoni (1991) have suggested that adolescence is also a period of
increasing empathy. Moreover, it appears that during adolescence
young persons more frequently recognize the value of helping others. Szagun (1992) has noted that when compared with younger

children, adolescents more commonly report being preoccupied with thoughts about others in distress and experiencing a desire to help them. This orientation yields direct personal and social benefits, since adolescents demonstrating cooperative and helpful behaviors tend to have higher self-esteem, to be more popular, and to exhibit less frequent problem behavior. Although in general females perceive themselves to be more helpful than males, with appropriate training in helping skills, males can also produce substantive social gains (Switzer et al. 1995). Although not yet extensive, research of this type suggests that the raw material of normal adolescence is sound and carries considerable helping potential.

REACHING BEYOND THE MILLENNIUM

More than ever before, schools are being perceived as agencies of change and development. This sea change in public perception clearly implies something more than academic change, since this in turn rests upon assumptions of orderly and cooperative behavior. Indeed, the British Government's Department for Education and Employment has determined that schools have a role in developing pupils' sense of responsibility and in promoting courtesy and consideration toward others (Department for Education and Employment 1994a). In order to match this aspiration, it follows that secondary schools should provide a caring lead for their student population. Another good reason for doing so is that caring for others is a fundamental goal underpinning any developed human society, and therefore one which it is desirable to model, transmit, and maintain between generations.

In practice, the delivery of effective caring may not be an easy assignment for today's schools however. There are several possible reasons for this. First, experienced teachers on both sides of the Atlantic have told the author that the nature of the school population has changed during the course of their career, notably in the direction of reduced student compliance. Second, it has recently been pointed out (Peel & Dansereau 1998) that typical educational programs do not provide teenagers with focused intervention on problem evaluation, on the identification of causes, on formulating optional responses, on calculating social costs, or on selecting the most productive alternatives. For many secondary students, performance on personal or interpersonal problem solving in school may therefore be as much a function of random or serendipitous social experience as it is a product of any educational influence.

Third, in light of their academic results becoming public domain information, it is understandable that schools have been found to exhibit downward pressure to improve test scores. Indeed, Bosworth (1995) suggests that this goal may have influenced teachers to emphasize the importance of traditional learning strategies to a degree that leaves little time for personalized interaction for their students. Secondary teachers in English schools have likewise informed the author that the current emphasis on delivering the National Curriculum has had considerable impact on their ability to engage in student-centered pastoral care activities.

Fourth, since most activities are organized by adults, it has been suggested that schools may offer little opportunity for most students to practice caring for others or to be recognized or rewarded for doing it. In addition, Bosworth reported from a year-long study of 300 classrooms that most interpersonal contacts appeared neutral in terms of the manifest level of caring involved. Such observations raise a question of how schools might be able to develop a more effective role in student support.

In keeping with the consumer orientation sustained throughout this text, it is interesting to note from Bosworth's research that students themselves put forward views constituting helpful guidance for education professionals. The most common theme to emerge from both male and female students in this study was that care involves both helping and empathy. Associated student values embraced kindness, respect, and loyalty, while key activities included listening, spending time together, and sharing personal experiences.

As far as student perceptions of teachers were concerned, Bosworth's students described caring teachers as listening, helping students to sort out relationship problems with their peers, providing advice and active assistance in setting goals, and staying after school to help with work or to talk about problems. Neither are such findings anomalous, insofar as they reinforce earlier work carried out by the author (Branwhite 1994) and student values indicated in the research data reported here. Because of the operational constraints imposed on teachers, however, schools wishing to provide opportunities for adolescents to learn and to demonstrate caring for others might well consider Bosworth's suggestion that the pool of persons able to contribute to this goal should be expanded. The present study demonstrates that the major human resource available to teachers is provided by secondary school students themselves.

THE DEVELOPMENT OF SCHOOL-BASED SERVICES

The ability to cope with the challenges of life and to help others in need is endemic to civilized society. Therefore, every school, as an agency of social values, has a key role to play in making sure that children develop both their coping and their helping potential. As a means to this end, caring schools are developing multilevel support systems that actively communicate concern for the welfare of others. This professional effort empowers secondary school teachers in achieving two important goals. First, it helps them to provide students with a functional model for coping with their own and with other people's problems. Second, it helps teachers to demonstrate the thinking needed to link aspirations of academic excellence with the reality of everyday adolescent experience.

While there are diverse proposals as to how either coping or helping ability might be developed, and a variety of approaches can be found in practice, child-centered policies appear to be a fundamental requirement. (A child-centered policy may be defined as one which is founded upon procedures for identifying and meeting children's needs.) Some authorities suggest that for maximum effectiveness, such a policy should ideally include preventative, early intervention, and developmental support functions.

At a *preventative* level, a child-centered policy sets out to minimize the occurrence of predictable problems (e.g., through establishing antibullying procedures). At an *early intervention* level, the policy should ensure a prompt response to the onset of significant problems (e.g., through investigating the causes of truancy). At a *developmental support* level, the policy accommodates persistent patterns of acute need (e.g., through seeking access to the resources of other agencies).

It has also been suggested that a caring school creates an atmosphere where all students can feel welcome, respected, and comfortable. (This naturally implies that some effort has been made to gather information about the nature of the relevant student perceptions.) For many neighborhood secondary schools, a caring culture is initially promoted by the way in which schools reach out to future students attending nearby feeder schools. Then, induction programs attempt to smooth the transition into secondary education. This caring culture is maintained through policies and procedures that promote student safety and well-being thereafter.

Nonetheless, research suggests that in the eyes of children, a caring school adds to the effect of its general policies by creating more specific interventions. It does so by creating opportunities for students to develop positive relationships with others; by providing appropriate guidance on how to take care of themselves and others; by encouraging students to contribute to the greater good via service to the school and its surrounding community; by providing age-appropriate recognition and reinforcement for cooperative or compliant behavior; and last, but not least, by adopting personalized approaches to solving student problems.

To provide excellent services for all students, schools necessarily need to maintain the quality of experience available to every individual. The pursuit of excellence is in itself an inclusive aim. In the nondiscriminatory context of a democratic school, that aim applies whether the students concerned are members of the majority who solve their problems without recourse to teacher support or are members of the minority who do seek out teacher resources.

Each group has differing needs, however, and therefore needs a different type of intervention. The majority group requires an emphasis on *indirect* care, designed to uphold and extend their existing coping skills. The minority group requires an emphasis on *direct* care that promotes shared responding. If there is any hint of a common thread connecting these differing interventions, then it is the superordinate goal of developing more effective solutions for student problems. Clearly however, neither majority-focused nor minority-focused interventions on their own can be considered adequate for meeting the goal of achieving excellence in student support. Only by combining the two approaches does the level of probability of success increase to an optimum level.

LEVEL OF PROVISION

The research reported here suggests that staffing resources for helping secondary school students to cope with individual or interpersonal difficulties could be planned on a rational criterion. The data from this investigation suggest that approximately 20 percent of adolescents experience personal problems for which they are likely to seek assistance in school. From the findings of this study, a neighborhood secondary school might therefore expect to have around 200 students in every 1,000 registered who may seek professional support because of self-related, interpersonal, or academic problems. This provides the English-school context with hard information about take-up rates for student support previously derived only from American and Scottish adolescents (Hutchinson & Bottorff 1986; Gray 1980).

INDIVIDUAL PROVISION

While the majority of the students may not have wanted teacher assistance for personal problems in the past, the reported survey data suggest that a significant number have nonetheless registered the existence of problems for which they would be likely to need help in the future. This is an area of fundamental importance, because personal, health, and social education (PHSE) programs as currently formulated cannot validly be expected to meet the needs of those students seeking adult support. For support purposes, most of the sample favored one-to-one meetings outside of the classroom, requiring individual exploration of their problems, feelings, options, and solutions. This form of support requires sensitivity, careful pacing, and an individually tailored approach on the part of the helper. In comparison, PHSE sessions are often classroom based, group focused, curriculum driven, and delivered at a rate which is in lock step with the school timetable. As presently constituted, they may therefore fall short of meeting identifiable aspirations of students who believe themselves to be in need of individual teacher support.

AVAILABILITY OF PROVISION

Another key feature of this investigation is that it pinpoints an adolescent need for rapid assistance, a fast-track requirement not picked up in single-site studies in English secondary schools. This sample of students made it clear that the majority wanted to wait only minutes for assistance with a personal problem. That time frame presents a relatively narrow window of opportunity, suggesting that to provide rapid access to helping resources, there may very well be a role for a walk-in advice center on each secondary school campus. For schools occupying a split site, it would appear desirable to set up more than one walk-in facility for the same reason.

HELPER CHARACTERISTICS

Given that the findings highlight a student need for same-age helpers, it also seems desirable to arrange for walk-in facilities to be served in the first instance by peer helpers rather than by teachers, although indirect professional supervision is clearly desirable. According to Shell and Eisenberg (1992) children are engaged in relationships that are asymmetric between generations, with rights and privileges interpreted by adults in their environment. In other words, there are likely to be closer parallels of experience within the same generation of students. Indeed, the work of Furman and Buhrmester (1985) incorporated reports from children indicating that they experienced more power in their relationships with other children than they did in relationships with adults. These observations reinforce the argument for appropriate peer level activity in the context of school support systems.

A more wide-ranging suggestion derives from the clear adolescent preference for friends as helpers. Indeed, given the survey evidence that adolescents are likely to experience multiple problems, it remains probable that friends will recurrently be asked for their support. Insofar as friendship is a normal feature of adolescence, then most secondary students can be regarded as potential helpers. In the student population, every school consequently has a sizable pool of helpers at its disposal, and harnessing this large-scale resource might reasonably be expected to enhance the availability of student support. Moreover, by educating all the students in solution-focused helping, schools may have at their disposal a large-scale mechanism for improving the climate of student interaction. Hence an integrated management plan for helping students to solve personal problems might be built upon a three-tier structure that facilitates the use of support from friends, from supervised peer helpers, and from professional sources available within the education service.

There is a caveat attached to this suggestion, however, which is derived directly from student opinion. Attempts to set up an integrated pattern of provision need to accommodate the finding that these three implicit levels of helping (i.e., from friends, peers, and professionals) are not given equal amounts of student support. Indeed, the results of this study show that a friend was the helper of first choice no less than fifty-seven times more often than other students and approximately twenty-four times more frequently than teachers or other professionals. Friends are by far the helpers of first choice, a preference that should therefore be reflected in the pattern of on-site provision.

It seems possible that this major divergence in helper preferences may have occurred because of varying frequency and quality of contact between those involved. Friendship offers a relationship that is founded upon repeated episodes of common experience, trust, intimacy, the sharing of deep personal thoughts or feelings, and successful conflict management (Gottman 1983; Roffey, Majors, & Tarrant 1997). Roffey et al. also argue that secondary school teachers are not well placed to be regarded as friends in the sense described because the positions of friendship and authority represent a contradiction in terms. This juxtaposition may perhaps help to explain why adolescents most frequently identify friends as their preferred helpers.

Nonetheless, in practice neither this nor any other explanation (such as the possibility that a threat to self-esteem is implicit in seeking help) should be taken to close off the possibility that friendly behavior on the part of teachers may exercise a positive influence on student perception or behavior. It also seems likely that friendly teachers are likely to be perceived as more empathic by their students and therefore more approachable in times of personal need. Friendly communication presents a positive form of social behavior that is also consistent with cultural norms within and between generations. It can therefore be recommended on several different grounds and adopted by teachers with good reason, provided we recognize that to be "friendly" does not imply that professionals will necessarily be viewed by students in the same way as friends.

While it has been shown that training teachers in counseling skills can enhance teacher–student relationships (Sakahura, Sano, & Fukushima 1993; Tojyo & Maeda 1993), from an adolescent standpoint the quality of student-to-student interaction remains the predominant issue. Moreover, as implied earlier, data from this survey do not favor the option of sustaining a future emphasis simply upon professionally delivered support. The findings suggest that while professional helpers may remain important for around 20 percent of the students, for the other 80 percent greater emphasis could be placed upon establishing indirect modes of support, for example, via supervision for friends or peers as helpers or through curriculum materials promoting greater personal and interpersonal effectiveness.

PEER INTERVENTION

From a professional perspective, recent research on peer counseling outcomes has indicated potential for helping with a variety of problems (see for example the work of Corn & Moore 1992; Deschesnes 1994; Gardner, & Martin 1989; Mather & Rutherford 1991; Quarmby 1993; Dolan 1995; Hendriksen 1991; Kim et al. 1992; Wang 1987). In the current educational climate, however, it is equally important to consider the student perspective, as this can provide a more sensitive test of how well professional constructions of reality meet the patterns of student need prevailing in real-world educational settings.

Findings from the present study reveal that for this random sample of secondary school students, peer helping, like its professional counterpart, received negligible adolescent support. This suggests that a degree of caution may be advisable before automatically choosing to implement conventional peer counseling programs as an initial response to student problems. The data show that less than 1 percent of the students favored other students as helpers, whereas 57 percent indicated that they preferred their friends in the role of helper. This finding is in accord with the view of Carter and Janzen (1994), who concluded that while secondary students often seek each other out for help, few indicate that they would actually seek help from a peer counselor. One implication of these data may be that student perceptions of trust are much stronger among friends. Moreover, the literature suggests that peer counselors have frequently been recruited from among white volunteers, which may be a discriminatory practice for schools operating in a multicultural setting. Accordingly, it appears that helping interventions should be built predominantly around friends as the agents of adolescent choice, given that the friendship network includes role models for supportive communication and action.

Two main lines of development follow for schools having an interest in peer support. First, in those schools that have already implemented some form of peer counseling program, further development could profitably be carried out to enhance student well-being. This would require expanding the existing vision to harness the potential of competent friends. Because of the widespread preference for friends as helpers documented here and elsewhere in the literature on adolescence, it would be constructive in the future to select potential peer counselors in the induction program on the basis of popularity among the other students in their age group. One reason for doing so is that popular peers are likely to be seen as friends by a greater number of students, and the frequency of student contact with peer counselors might therefore be expected to increase. An objective procedure for identifying the popularity of potential peer counselors may be found in the administration of sociograms within existing teaching groups, although teacher observation could also be useful in assessing the likely appeal and viability of peer counseling volunteers.

Second, for schools that have not yet begun a peer counseling program as such, there is now a professionally justifiable alternative of choosing not to do so. This suggestion is again made on the basis of the predominant student preference for friends as helpers. Accordingly, student support could quite reasonably be fostered by focusing upon friends as the most readily available supportive resource and setting out to enhance their helping skills, although this would clearly imply greater care than a simple befriending program would be likely to need.

By pursuing this option, a school could still enhance its level of student support, but would not have to set up a peer counseling system per se. This opens up creative possibilities which offer exciting new potential. For any school deciding not to introduce peer counseling, the entry level of student support can immediately be recognized as less discriminatory, since it does not involve teachers in selecting an exclusive cohort of peer counselors. Rather, the school sets out to provide excellent support through delivering key helper skills to *all* students. By doing so it would be demonstrating to students, parents, administrators, politicians, and the wider community the importance that is being attached to an inclusive approach to student concerns.

CURRICULUM-BASED INTERVENTION

Enhancing the role of friends as helpers would necessarily require a group level of intervention, partly because of the numbers of students involved. This in turn suggests that a curriculum-based approach could be beneficial at a preventative level. Although the personal, health, and social education curriculum is clearly no substitute for student-requested individual help, its particular value is that of assisting the vast majority of students (identified in this study as independent problem solvers) to develop their coping and helping potential. Moreover, it is not beyond the bounds of possibility that the minority of students (identified here as those seeking teacher support) could also have their skills enhanced through a curriculum that sets out to enhance the application of their emotional intelligence.

While considerable development of the existing PHSE curriculum would probably be necessary to achieve this goal, a curriculum-based approach could prove an efficient mechanism for future development. One reason for this is that within a given time frame more students are likely to learn the relevant concepts and strategies than any one-on-one intervention could possibly hope to provide. Another is that shared learning experiences are more likely to achieve the critical mass necessary to accelerate change on the scale required to create a significant shift in the caring climate of any school concerned.

What might the main framework of an effective curriculum-driven intervention need to include? The most critical components of any helping curriculum are necessarily those that meet the stated needs of the student population. In order to reflect a process of solution-focused intervention, this student sample shows that it is essential to embrace two distinct but related levels of information. The first level addresses strategies for dealing with problems, whereas the second level focuses on strategies for shifting problem processing into solution processing. Related areas that it could be helpful to cover include emotional and social coping skills, maintaining self-esteem, problem solving, and conflict resolution. Some investigators believe that acquisition and maintenance of specific skill domains, such as communication skills, thinking skills, and decision-making skills, would also make a formative contribution.

Communication skills would predictably need to embrace three areas. The first of these requires development of the essential descriptive vocabulary and the language skills for putting feelings into appropriate words. The second involves the development of existing inner dialogue to control negative thoughts and to augment current coping ability. The third demands the development of accurate listening skills for understanding others and establishing a functional interaction with them.

Coverage of thinking skills would in turn need to incorporate two separate tracks. One of these would deal with slowing down or stopping certain affective or cognitive events. The other would deal with increasing the flow of thoughts and images that empower the individual student. Here, the slow track promotes the control of self-disabling thoughts and images, of otherwise impulsive behaviors, and of potential outbursts of destructive anger. The fast track aims to raise motivation, increase effort, recall past successes, review helpful influences, and build future goals. The key function served by both tracks is to drive overt and covert activities designed to make challenging personal or interpersonal situations better.

Inclusion of decision-making skills is needed to help with basic issues like the analysis of who owns a given problem, who could help in resolving it, and how soon action is needed. It also bears on issues like what kind of response might be acceptable and what behavior would be unacceptable. It considers which possible reactions could be helpful and which actions unhelpful. It balances when would be a good time to initiate action against when is likely to be a bad time. Decision-making skills are also important in specifying a goal that is achievable; and in identifying alternative pathways for bridging the divide between that goal and the current problem. Last, but not least, decision-making skills would also help to identify desirable outcomes, both from the point of view of others and from that of the student concerned.

SOLUTION-FOCUSED INTERVENTION

This study clearly demonstrates the acceptability of solution-focused approaches for secondary students, and it does so in two main ways. The first of these is through showing that the majority of the total student sample believed it important to explore alternative options and proposed solutions. The second was by showing that exposure to interventions including solution-focused elements met with a high level of recipient approval.

Support for a solution-focused approach to helping adolescents is provided by Durrant (1995), who provides a readable outline of what can be achieved regarding school-related problems. Additional backing is given by Littrell, Malia, and Vanderwood (1995), who point out that because of the number of students whom school-based helpers are likely to serve, time-limited approaches are needed. In their study, helpers were able to reduce the amount of contact time needed when using a solution-focused intervention.

These authors also point out that considerable skill is required to help students establish small and meaningful goals and to set tasks related to the achievement of those goals. In order to make the goals and related tasks manageable, however, it is desirable that they should be reviewed in the context of existing coping skills in order to facilitate the growth of student understanding, confidence, and motivation. In solution-focused helping, it is important that existing coping skills are mapped out through the exploration of the exceptions created by problem-managed, problem-reduced, or problem-free areas of the student's experience. The search for exceptions is of crucial importance because it can provide indications of self-control existing within two separate domains. The most obvious of these can be found in signs of restraint already existent within the student's behavior.

No less significant is any indication that *cognitive* controls are being exercised. Cognitive controls can often be detected by listing the student's self-statements and associated visual imagery. In particular it is important to access adolescent notions of worth and care, relating either to the self or to others, because these provide a meaningful foundation for engaging the student in a process of change. Cognitive controls are potentially empowering for students experiencing personal problems, because they can be used not only to moderate internal and external behavior, but may also be applied when visualizing a more desirable future.

To create and maintain change in an acceptable direction, it is clear that both overt and covert activities make a formative contribution. This shared contribution of behavior and cognition underpins a whole spectrum of change and development that can be implemented in the context of school-based helping. The extent to which schools can make headway in this area is of course dependent upon good leadership and the professionalism of teachers, many of whom possess an extensive range of interpersonal and decision-making skills.

For schools interested in developing solution-focused student support, some useful indicators to consider include these items:

- Teachers provide a positive role model in searching for solutions.
- Teachers instruct students in problem-solving skills.

- Teachers emphasize the importance of the future rather than the past.
- Teachers identify coping rather than failing behaviors.
- Teachers seek out change rather than sameness.
- Teachers search for goals rather than motives.
- Teachers actively invoke students' solutions.
- Teachers help students to work toward a solution promptly.
- Teachers coach students to take small steps toward an agreed future goal.
- Teachers actively encourage students to create additional solutions.
- Teachers actively encourage students to help others construct solutions.
- Teachers support each other's attempts to design solutions.

Any school program that already utilizes the majority of these indicators could quite reasonably compliment itself on having given a high priority to achieving solution-focused student support and could maintain this achievement by doing more of what is already known to work for its own community.

SERVICE DELIVERY ISSUES

Results from this study indicate that students commonly report multiple problems. It also reveals that although most students draw on the resources of their friends, a significant number nonetheless approach teachers for help. This finding suggests that integrated planning should be regarded as a critical function for teachers providing on-site student support, so that their additional skills can be applied where the need is greatest.

As far as individual helping is concerned, teachers need to be aware of a student desire to talk about their problems and their feelings promptly, to be listened to, to receive suggestions for their future options and potential solutions, and to have their concerns addressed in confidence. It should also be a salutary reminder to have regard for those findings indicating that the use of students' first names, pertinent helper self-disclosure, positive helper feedback, and exploration of their existing coping skills were reported by only a minority of these adolescents. Some development of school-based helping would therefore open up the possibility that a greater number of students could benefit from more frequent application of these particular techniques. Achieving this goal may also help teachers to reduce the likelihood of students experiencing a sense of threat to their self-esteem when seeking help in school.

The data which demonstrate that while students had multiple problems the majority did not seek help from teachers can be taken to further imply that at least some professional time should be given to modes of teacher intervention that are not constrained to one-to-one helping. Fortunately, there are several alternative modes of intervention available, in addition to the curriculum-based activities discussed earlier. One option would be setting up a screening program to determine levels of need among existing students, particularly first-time arrivals. Another might be to establish referral procedures that filter out low-level problems which could be handled by others, so that professional expertise can be applied to more acute levels of need in an optimum manner. A logical extension of this would involve setting up partnerships with other teachers and psychologists to establish a program to develop student self-help.

STAFF DEVELOPMENT

Although the view of the Office for Standards in Education (1994) is that some teachers need to improve their counseling skills, the lack of time that teachers have to do this is not the only obstacle to overcome in creating an effective provision for student support. Reid (1989) points out that teachers are not initially trained to understand such issues as age and sex appropriateness of behavior; life circumstances; extent of disturbance; type, severity, or frequency of symptoms; aspects of diagnosis and prognosis; links with mental retardation; or classification, unusualness, or conformity. Moreover, Wade and Moore (1993) found that less than one-third of 115 teachers whom they surveyed reported taking any account of the opinions of the children they taught.

Current evidence suggests that there is a necessity for further refinement of student support in order to meet existing levels of need. This is likely to require new training initiatives, and in the writer's experience, such training appears most effective when delivered by professionals familiar with the schools as well as with appropriate theory and intervention techniques. Indeed, it appears that there may be a constructive role here for psychologists employed in the education service to provide cost-effective research, consultation, and training for staff with helping responsibilities. Moreover, provision of extensive training or a large number of staff development sessions may need the combined resources of several professionals.

One of the basic principles for organizing staff training should be that it assists teachers in insuring that their professional time is used as effectively as possible. It is therefore suggested that training programs should include both preventative and supportive elements. The preventative element would need to be set in the context of whole-school behavior and discipline policies. Against that background, it seems desirable to develop and implement more effective programs for student induction and to establish utilitarian skills for coping with the demands of the school environment.

To complement this approach, the supportive element should include establishing both student- and teacher-support systems in order to accommodate those students needing help in coping with personal concerns. From the results of this study, both student- and teacher-delivered support could be built around a basic package of skills in listening, building rapport, identifying personal resources, and exploring future options and potential solutions. For teacher intervention, however, training inputs should also include coverage of relevant implementation and monitoring skills. The provision of relevant guidance for involving or referring to other professionals also appears desirable.

Delivery of a comprehensive in-service training program designed to encompass these elements would probably require the resources of personnel with appropriate background in enhancing self-esteem, adolescent coping, problem solving, counseling, and solution-focused helping. The development of a joint approach that involves teachers and relevant support services may be particularly productive in realizing these goals.

QUALITY ISSUES

For planning purposes it is clearly desirable to find out from students what they would like a personal support service to deliver in their own school. Once these data are available (e.g., from a survey of the student population), management of a needs-based support system is likely to become better informed and therefore make more effective use of the staff who have been trained in service implementation and delivery. In order to achieve consistency of service, it also seems advisable to formulate clear and concise staff guidelines and relevant support materials and to supplement appropriate professional training with a system of recording how the service is used and delivered.

Use of meaningful evaluation sheets by service users should be encouraged to provide up-to-date feedback on relevant success factors and changing patterns of student perception and experience. For the sake of efficiency it is desirable to maintain records of the work undertaken that are clear, simple, and require a minimum of time to complete. Data recording may vary in certain respects from school to school. Aspects like who makes use of the service provided, why they do so, whom they get in touch with, the frequency and duration of contact, an outline of the intervention, and what students found helpful are, however, fairly basic requirements. Access to a computer system running a Windows-driven database could provide a relatively user-friendly management information system that is capable of providing summary data at the touch of a button. A regular internal review cycle based upon the summarized performance data would help to inform decision making regarding future service development.

To help schools that are committed to the development of excellent student support services, relevant indicators to consider include these items.

- An established induction process for all new students.
- Labeling and resourcing of places of safety on the school campus.
- Making support guidelines accessible to all students, including those with reading disabilities.
- Routine student involvement in developing support materials and procedures.
- The availability of focused curriculum materials.
- The availability of student formats for opinion-survey and problem-solving purposes.
- A published student-support policy which specifies professional responsibilities.
- A clear process for disseminating related information to teachers and parents.
- Implementation of an appropriate school-wide record-keeping system.
- Explanatory information and progress reports for parents and other interested parties.
- Development of an enhanced parent involvement program.
- Evidence of an internal monitoring process that includes an annual review cycle.

While these items are neither exhaustive nor listed in any particular order of importance, it is anticipated that they should help caring schools (in partnership with students, with parents, and with other education professionals) in the task of enhancing at least some aspects of their existing student support provision.

FUNDING ISSUES

From the point of view of funding the necessary development, the allocation of school resources for student support should be founded upon the recognition that student needs are by no means restricted to academic issues. It would therefore seem reasonable that a proportion of available funds should go toward assisting staff to meet students' need for personal support by establishing appropriate whole-school approaches in keeping with identified patterns of student need. Although there would be an inevitable cost involved in providing a multilevel service, this may be offset in the longer term by influencing other attributes of the school, such as the climate of student interaction, frequency of conflict, attendance levels, or perceived teacher stress.

In the case of secondary schools operating in areas where the student population indicates a particularly high level of need, the case may be stronger for establishing an integrated program with neighborhood feeder schools. Alternatively, it may be desirable to share costs between secondary schools, to seek help from partnerships within the local community, or perhaps to make joint representations for special-purpose funding from central sources. For rapid cost-effectiveness, it may prove desirable to adopt an approach that focuses initially on enhancing student-delivered support, which looks at ways of sharing materials or staff time between secondary schools and which makes more strategic use of relevant existing expertise among support service personnel.

SUPPORT SERVICE PARTNERSHIPS

In today's educational climate, it is clear that there is a need for schools to develop effective partnerships with their support services if they are to deliver the high quality of educational experience that all students have a right to expect. Given that most students spend over a decade progressing through the school system and encounter some significant challenges during that time, some will exhibit levels of need that cannot be met solely through the resources of the school. Moreover, some of the problems occurring may be sufficiently complex that they require input from a number of support services in order to receive adequate attention.

An important consideration here is that of the role psychologists may usefully adopt to support the improvement of school-based services. One significant gain to be derived from consulting the school's psychologist is that this can provide access to a view that is not constrained by reductionist concerns with only one area of student activity. Psychologists working in the education service necessarily deal with a broader definition of reality. Whilst having a pragmatic awareness of school-related concerns, they also offer expertise which, uniquely among education professionals, is based upon scientific knowledge of human performance, mental health, and organizational issues. This human resource offers sufficient flexibility that can be applied at various levels of the school community and across a variety of student numbers or needs. Moreover, it provides another means for schools to demonstrate that they deliver added value for their student population.

For example, by applying their training in research skills, psychologists can help teachers to sample student opinion with a minimum of effort. By drawing upon their knowledge of instructional psychology, they can help to design more effective curriculum materials. By using their knowledge of therapeutic interventions, they can help skilled teachers reduce the impact of student problems. By invoking their understanding of conflict resolution, they can assist teaching colleagues to cut down the number of incidents of victimization. By employing their background in behavioral science, they can help schools to develop more effective discipline policies for promoting positive and productive student activity. By engaging their understanding of family processes, they can support schools in developing more inclusive parent-involvement programs. Such possibilities clearly contain a number of useful options for schools to consider.

DIRECTIONS FOR FUTURE RESEARCH

A number of aspects of the work undertaken merit further investigation. Not the least of these is the need to gather data from students from other cultures and contexts. It would also be helpful to further the course of inquiry by examining both the consistency and variability of adolescent coping behaviors across a range of personal problems. In addition, little is known about which helping statements or behaviors of friends are regarded as being most effective. It may also be useful, in terms of planning student support, to ask secondary students who have sought help in school what the sequence of interventions is that they would like to have provided, a question that was not resolved within the present research. The results also strongly suggest that the utility of peer support and helper programs should also be closely researched from a consumer perspective. Furthermore, there is a place for longitudinal studies to assess the impact of student opinion upon the practice of teachers, counselors, and other professional helpers if progress in this area is to be maintained.

Information-emphasis approaches to helping adolescents (such as that implicit in personal, health, and social education programs) also need student-focused evaluation to determine the extent to which the topics covered are appropriate for meeting their needs.

The development and evaluation of some form of expert system technology for student support purposes should also prove constructive. This already exists in certain contexts such as career guidance, where computer programs can guide students through complex decisions, while offering an emotionally neutral and individually paced technology that may also have a constructive role to play in augmenting personal problem-solving strategies.

More studies are urgently needed to build up a comprehensive body of knowledge about adolescent reactions to helping interventions. For example, the development of knowledge regarding the influence of somatic reactions and self-statements at different stages of the helping process would help to fill significant gaps in the adolescent literature. Given that secondary school students have been found to be significantly less self-disclosing than college students (Snoek & Rothblum 1979), future research needs to look specifically at the needs of adolescents in the school system.

It might well be argued that present practice appears to undervalue the viewpoint of those very students who are the de facto end users of educational services. From this it follows that in the absence of change, persisting disparity between professional practice and the perspectives of secondary school students provides grounds for genuine concern. In light of recent research, the time appears ripe to reexamine the validity of traditional approaches to student support.

There appears to be some need to refine existing approaches by establishing an educational reality that is more closely attuned to the needs of adolescents. The gain to be derived from meeting this need is that present and future generations of adolescents could then experience more consistent and robust combinations of personal well-being, social value, and academic success in school. The added value of high quality educational experience which meets students' personal needs is likely to develop in the student a more secure foundation upon which to base a positive social contribution and to prepare for the later responsibilities of adult life.

Appendix:
Survey Questionnaire

STUDENT HELP FORM
(PART ONE: PERSONAL DETAILS)

SCHOOL: .... SEX: .... AGE: ......

YEAR: .... CLASS: ....

1.1 How do you like to spend most of your time?

(TICK <u>ONE</u> CHOICE)

☐ Alone ☐ With your Family ☐ With Friends ☐ Don't Know

1.2 How many personal problems do you think that you have?

(TICK <u>ONE</u> CHOICE)

☐ None ☐ A Few ☐ A Lot ☐ Don't Know

1.3 When you have a personal problem how do you usually react at first?

(TICK <u>ONE</u> CHOICE)

☐ Worry about it ☐ Laugh about it

☐ Get angry ☐ Cry

☐ Think about something else ☐ Tell yourself it could be worse

☐ Don't Know

1.4 When you have a personal problem, what do you usually do about it later?

(TICK <u>ONE</u> CHOICE)

☐ Do nothing ☐ Try to solve the problem yourself

☐ Ask someone else to help you solve it ☐ Ask someone else to solve it for you

☐ Don't Know

1.5 What kind of personal problems would you be most likely to need help with:

(TICK THE ITEMS THAT ARE CORRECT FOR YOU)

A problem about your:-

	Likely	Not Likely	Don't Know		Likely	Not Likely	Don't Know
FEELINGS	☐	☐	☐	RELATIONSHIPS	☐	☐	☐
LOOKS	☐	☐	☐	MONEY	☐	☐	☐
MIND	☐	☐	☐	SEX	☐	☐	☐
BODY	☐	☐	☐	DRUGS	☐	☐	☐
DREAMS	☐	☐	☐	TEACHERS	☐	☐	☐
RELIGION	☐	☐	☐	SCHOOLWORK	☐	☐	☐
BULLYING	☐	☐	☐	CAREER	☐	☐	☐

1.6 How many personal problems have you solved without help from someone else?

(TICK ONE CHOICE)

☐ A lot   ☐ Some   ☐ Very Few

☐ None   ☐ Don't Know

STUDENT HELP FORM
(PART TWO: SCHOOL INFORMATION)

(PLEASE TICK <u>ONE</u> BOX FOR EACH QUESTION)

2.1   Is it possible to get help with personal problems in your school?

☐ Yes   ☐ No   ☐ Don't Know

2.2   Who would you go to for this kind of help in school?

☐ Form Tutor   ☐ Subject Teacher   ☐ Head of Year

☐ Deputy Head   ☐ Head Teacher   ☐ Someone Else

☐ Secretary   ☐ Doctor   ☐ Don't Know

2.3   How easily do you get to see the person ticked in question 2.2?

☐ Easily   ☐ With difficulty

☐ Very easily   ☐ With great difficulty   ☐ Don't Know

2.4   How long would you expect to wait to get help, after you have asked for it?

☐ Minutes   ☐ Hours   ☐ Days   ☐ Weeks   ☐ Don't Know

2.5   While you have been at this school, have you ever WANTED a teacher to talk one of your problems over with you?

☐ Often   ☐ Sometimes   ☐ Rarely   ☐ Never   ☐ Don't Know

2.6   While you have been at this school, have you ever ASKED a teacher to talk one of your problems over with you?

☐ Often   ☐ Sometimes   ☐ Rarely   ☐ Never   ☐ Don't Know

125

2.7 If you ticked OFTEN, SOMETIMES or RARELY in Question 2.6, how long after the problem started did you wait before asking for help?

☐ Minutes ☐ Hours ☐ Days ☐ Weeks ☐ Don't Know

2.8 Have you received help with a personal problem in school yourself?

(TICK THE CORRECT BOX)

YES	
NO	

If you ticked "YES", go to part **Four** now

If you ticked "NO", go to part **Three** now

STUDENT HELP FORM
(PART THREE: PERSONAL REFERENCES)

FILL IN PART THREE IF YOU HAVE NOT BEEN GIVEN HELP WITH A PERSONAL PROBLEM

3.1 If you need help, who would you prefer to help you with a personal problem?

(A) (TICK ONE PERSON HERE)

☐ A Friend ☐ Another Student ☐ A Teacher

☐ Another Professional Person ☐ A Parent of a Friend ☐ One of your own Parents

☐ Someone Else ☐ Don't Know

(B) (TICK ONE PERSON HERE)

☐ Someone Younger ☐ Someone your own age ☐ Someone a little older

☐ Someone a lot older ☐ Don't Know

(C) (TICK ONE PERSON HERE)

☐ Someone of the same sex as yourself ☐ Someone of the opposite sex ☐ Don't Know

3.2 If you had to choose a teacher, whom would you prefer to help you with a personal problem?

(TICK ONE PERSON)

☐ Form Tutor ☐ Subject Teacher ☐ Head of Year

☐ Deputy Head ☐ Head Teacher ☐ Don't Know

3.3 How would you prefer this person to find out about your problem?

(TICK ONE CHOICE)

☐ From You ☐ From a Teacher ☐ From a Friend

☐ From Your Family ☐ Don't Know

☐ By Letter   ☐ By Telephone   ☐ From Face-to-Face Meeting

☐ Don't Know

3.4 HOW would you prefer to meet this person?

(TICK <u>ONE</u> CHOICE)

☐ On your own   ☐ With a friend   ☐ With a parent/guardian

☐ With your whole family   ☐ In a group of students with personal problems   ☐ Don't Know

3.5 WHERE would you prefer to meet a helper?

(TICK <u>ONE</u> CHOICE)

☐ In a classroom   ☐ In a corridor   ☐ In a school office

☐ In the school library   ☐ At home   ☐ Don't Know

3.6 WHEN would you prefer to meet a helper?

(TICK <u>ONE</u> CHOICE)

☐ Before school starts   ☐ During lessons   ☐ Morning break

☐ Lunchtime   ☐ Afternoon break   ☐ After school

☐ Evening   ☐ Don't Know

3.7 In what ways would you like a helper to assist you to START talking?

(TICK <u>ONE OR MORE</u> CHOICES)

☐ Greeting you   ☐ Using your first name   ☐ Saying something nice about you

☐ Asking you what is the matter   ☐ Waiting for you to speak   ☐ Don't Know

128

3.8 In what way would you like a helper to assist you to describe a personal PROBLEM?

(TICK <u>ONE OR MORE</u> CHOICES)

☐ Asking you if you have a problem

☐ Asking you to talk about your problem

☐ Asking you questions about your problem

☐ Something else

☐ Don't Know

3.9 In what ways would you like a helper to assist you to describe your FEELINGS?

(TICK <u>ONE OR MORE</u> CHOICES)

By:-

☐ Asking you how you feel

☐ Asking if you have told anyone else about your feelings

☐ Asking you questions about your feelings

☐ Something else

☐ Don't Know

3.10 In what ways would you like a helper to assist you to work out your options?

(TICK <u>ONE OR MORE</u> CHOICES)

☐ Describing your problem in a few words

☐ Telling you not to worry

☐ Asking for your ideas

☐ Giving you some suggestions

☐ Something else

☐ Don't Know

3.11 How would you like a helper to assist you to create a possible SOLUTION for your problems?

(TICK <u>ONE OR MORE</u> CHOICES)

☐ Asking if you know a possible solution

☐ Asking how you have solved other problems

☐ Suggesting a possible solution

☐ Something else

☐ Don't Know

3.12 What might make you decide to STOP meeting with an adult who was trying to help you?

(TICK ONE OR MORE CHOICES)

☐ Times not convenient   ☐ Questions too personal   ☐ Too many questions

☐ Too much help given   ☐ Not enough help given   ☐ Telling someone else what you said

☐ Something else   ☐ Problem stopped   ☐ Don't Know

3.13 What would you FIRST suggest to a school friend with a personal problem about getting help?

(TICK ONE CHOICE)

☐ Ask a Teacher   ☐ Ask a Friend   ☐ Ask a Parent

☐ Call Childline   ☐ Write to a Magazine   ☐ Don't Know

(FILL IN PART **FOUR** IF YOU <u>HAVE</u> BEEN GIVEN HELP WITH A PERSONAL PROBLEM)

4.1   When you talked your problems over with a teacher was it because

(TICK <u>ONE</u> CHOICE)

☐ You decided to do so yourself   ☐ A Friend said you should

☐ A Parent said you should   ☐ Another Teacher said you should   ☐ Don't Know

4.2   When you talked your problems over with a teacher, what did they do to help you to START talking?

(TICK <u>ONE OR MORE</u> CHOICES)

☐ Greeted You   ☐ Used your first name

☐ Said something nice about you   ☐ Asked you about yourself   ☐ Don't Know

4.3   When you talked your problems over with a teacher, what did they do that showed they were LISTENING to what you said?

(TICK <u>ONE OR MORE</u> CHOICES)

☐ Looked at you   ☐ Nodded their head

☐ Asked related questions   ☐ Looked interested   ☐ Don't Know

4.4   When you talked your problems over with a teacher, what did they do to help you describe a personal problem?

(TICK <u>ONE OR MORE</u> CHOICES)

☐ Asked if you had a problem   ☐ Asked you to talk about your problem

☐ Asked you questions about your problem   ☐ Something else   ☐ Don't Know

131

4.5　When you talked your problems over with a teacher, what did they do that told you they were trying to understand your FEELINGS?

(TICK <u>ONE OR MORE</u> CHOICES)

☐ Asked how you felt

☐ Asked if you had told anyone else about your feelings

☐ Asked you questions about your problem

☐ Something else

☐ Don't Know

4.6　When you talked your problems over with a teacher, what did they do that helped you to feel more AT EASE?

(TICK <u>ONE OR MORE</u> CHOICES)

☐ Said that they would help

☐ Told you not to worry

☐ Told you about a similar problem of their own

☐ Something else

☐ Don't Know

4.7　When you talked your problem over with a teacher, what did they do that helped you to understand there were ALTERNATIVE ways to handle the problem?

(TICK <u>ONE OR MORE</u> CHOICES)

☐ Described your problem in a few words

☐ Told you not to worry

☐ Asked about your ideas

☐ Gave you some suggestions

☐ Something else

☐ Don't Know

4.8　When you talked your problems over with a teacher, what did they do that helped to create a possible SOLUTION for your problem?

TICK <u>ONE OR MORE</u> CHOICES)

☐ Asked if you knew a possible solution

☐ Asked how you had solved other problems

☐ Suggested a possible solution

☐ Something else

☐ Don't Know

4.9   How much of the help that you were given was the kind of help that you
      EXPECTED?

      (TICK ONE CHOICE)

      ☐ All of it   ☐ Most of it   ☐ Asked about your
                                                      ideas

      ☐ A little of it   ☐ None of it   ☐ Don't Know

4.10 How would you DESCRIBE the kind of help that you were given?

      (TICK ONE CHOICE)

      ☐ Very helpful   ☐ Quite helpful
      ☐ OK   ☐ Not helpful   ☐ Don't Know

4.11 What happened to the problem AFTER you got help?

      (TICK ONE CHOICE)

      ☐ It went away completely   ☐ It got better but did not go away

      ☐ It stayed the same   ☐ It went away for a while but came back

      ☐ It caused other problems   ☐ It got worse

                                   ☐ Don't Know

4.12 Did the help you were given assist you with any OTHER problems?

      (TICK ONE CHOICE)

      ☐ Yes, with an old problem   ☐ Yes, with a new problem that started
        that you did not talk about   since you got help

      ☐ No, it did not help with other ☐ Don't Know
        problems

133

4.13   What was it easy for you to talk about?

(TICK <u>ONE OR MORE</u> CHOICES)

☐ Feelings	☐ Looks	☐ Religion
☐ Body	☐ Dreams	☐ Sex
☐ Relationships	☐ Money	☐ School Work
☐ Drugs	☐ Teachers	☐ Bullying
☐ Career	☐ Mind	☐ Don't Know

4.14   What was it HARD for you to talk about?

(TICK <u>ONE OR MORE</u> CHOICES)

☐ Feelings	☐ Looks	☐ Religion
☐ Body	☐ Dreams	☐ Sex
☐ Relationships	☐ Money	☐ School Work
☐ Drugs	☐ Teachers	☐ Bullying
☐ Career	☐ Mind	☐ Don't Know

THANK YOU FOR FILLING IN THIS FORM

© TONY BRANWHITE PhD

Bibliography

Items are included in this bibliography either because they are directly referred to in the text or because they provided helpful background reading for the author.

Abal, K., & Hornby, G. (1995). "Perceptions of the educational counsellor's role in Kuwaiti secondary schools." *International Journal for the Advancement of Counseling* 17: 249–262.

Abbott, K., Tollefson, N., & McDermott, D. (1982). "Counsellor race as a factor in counselor preference." *Journal of College Student Personnel* 23: 36–40.

Abel, H., & Gingles, R. (1965). "Identifying problems of adolescent girls." *Journal of Educational Research* 58(9): 389–393.

Achenbach, T. M., & Edelbrock, C. (1987). "Manual for the youth self-report and profile." Burlington, VT: University of Vermont, Department of Psychiatry.

Acosta, F. X. (1980). "Self-described reasons for premature termination of psychotherapy by Mexican American, Black American, and Anglo-American patients." *Psychological Reports* 47: 435–443.

Adams, J. S. (1963). "Towards an understanding of inequity." *Journal of Abnormal and Social Psychology* 67: 422–436.

Adams, M., & Adams, J. (1991). "Life events, depression, and perceived problem-solving alternatives in adolescence." *Journal of Child Psychology and Psychiatry* 32: 811–820.

Adelman, H. S., Barker, L. A., & Nelson, P. (1993). "A study of a school-based clinic: Who uses it and who doesn't?" *Journal of Clinical Child Psychology* 22(1): 52–59.

Adelman, H. S., MacDonald, V. M., Nelson, P., Smith, D. C., & Taylor, L. (1990). "Motivational readiness and the participation of children with learning and behaviour problems in psychoeducational decision-making." *Journal of Learning Disabilities* 23(3): 171–176.

Adelman, H. S., & Taylor, L. (1986). "Children's reluctance during treatment: Incompetence, resistance, or an appropriate response?" *School Psychology Review* 15(1): 91–99. EJ330742.

Alexander, L., & Luborsky, L. (1984). "Research on the helping alliance." In L. Greenberg & W. Pinsof (Eds.), *The Psychotherapeutic Process: A Research Handbook*. New York: Guilford.

Alexy, W. D. (1982). "Dimensions of psychological counseling that facilitate the grieving process of bereaved parents." *Journal of Counseling Psychology* 29(5): 498–507.

Altmann, H., & Firnesz, K. (1973). "A role-playing appproach to influencing behavioural change and self-esteem." *Elementary School Guidance and Counseling* 7: 276–281.

Amanant, E. (1979). "Paradoxical treatment of adolescent resistance." *Adolescence* 14: 851–855.

Amato, P. R., & Bradshaw, R. (1985). "An exploratory study of people's reasons for delaying or avoiding help-seeking." *Australian Psychologist* 20(1): 21–23.

Amato, P. R., & Saunders, J. (1985). "The perceived dimensions of help-seeking." *Social Psychology Quarterly* 48(2): 130–137.

American Psychological Association. (1994). *Publication Manual of the American Psychological Association*. Washington, DC: American Psychological Association.

Ammerman, M. S., & Fryear, J. L. (1975). "Photographic enhancement of children's self-esteem." *Psychology in the Schools* 12: 319–325.

Andert, J. N. (1978). *You've gotta keep the customer satisfied: Assessing client satisfaction*. Paper presented at the annual convention of the American Psychological Association, Toronto. ED163381.

Andrews, W. R. (1971). "Behavioural and client-centered counseling of high-school under-achievers." *Journal of Counseling Psychology* 18: 93–96.

Ansubel, D. P., Montmeyor, R., & Svajian, P. N. (1977). *Theory and Problems of Adolescent Development* (2d ed.). New York: Grune & Stratton.

Apostal, R. A. (1968). "Comparison of counselors and non-counselors with type of problem controlled." *Journal of Counseling Psychology* 15: 407–410.

Archer, J. (1984). "Waiting list dropouts in a university counseling center." *Professional Psychology: Research and Practice* 15(3): 388–395.

Armacost, R. L. (1989). "Perceptions of stressors by high-school students." *Journal of Adolescent Research* 4(4): 443–461.

———. (1990). "High school student stress and the role of counselors." *The School Counselor* 38: 105–112.

Armsden, G. C., & Greenberg, M. T. (1987). "The inventory of parent and peer attachment: Individual differences and their relationship to psychological well-being in adolescence." *Journal of Youth and Adolescence* 16(5): 427–435.

Arnold, J., Budd, R. J., & Miller, K. (1988). "Young peoples' perceptions of the uses and usefulness of different sources of careers help." *British Journal of Guidance and Counselling* 16(1): 83–89.

Arulsigamoni, A. (1972). *The relationship between self-concept and school achievement in low achieving junior high-school children*. Ph.D. dissertation, American University.

Atkinson, D. R. (1983). "Ethnic similarity in counseling psychology." *Counseling Psychologist* 11: 79–92.

Atkinson, D. R., Brady, S., & Casas, J. M. (1981). "Sexual preference similarity, attitude similarity, and perceived counselor credibility and attractiveness." *Journal of Counseling Psychology* 28: 504–509.

Atkinson, D. R., Furlong, M. J., & Poston, W. C. (1986). "Afro-American preferences for counselor characteristics." *Journal of Counseling Psychology* 33(3): 326–330.

Atkinson, D. R., Jennings, R. G., & Liongson, L. (1990). "Minority students reasons for not seeking counseling and suggestions for improving services." *Journal of College Student Development* 31: 342–350.

Atkinson, D. R., Maruyama, M., & Matsui, S. (1978). "Effects of counselor race and counselor approach on Asian Americans' perceptions of counselor credulity and utility." *Journal of Counseling Psychology* 25: 76–83.

Atkinson, D. R., Ponterotto, J. G., & Sanchez, A. R. (1984). "Attitudes of Vietnamese and Anglo-American students towards counseling." *Journal of College Student Personnel* (September): 448–452.

Atkinson, D. R., Poston, W. C., & Furlong, M. J. (1989). "Ethnic group preferences for counselor characteristics." *Journal of Counseling Psychology* 36(1): 68–72.

Atkinson, D. R., & Schein, S. (1986). "Similarity in counseling." *The Counseling Psychologist* 14(4): 319–354.

Azim, H.F.A., & Joyce, M. A. (1986). "The impact of data-based program modifications on the satisfaction of outpatients in group psychotherapy." *Canadian Journal of Psychiatry* 31: 119–122.

Bachelor, A. (1988). "How clients perceive therapist empathy: A content analysis of received empathy." *Psychotherapy* 25(2): 227–240.

Barabasz, A. F. (1972). "A comparative study of counselee preferences for behaviourist and client-centered counseling approaches." *Child Study Journal* 2(3): 117–122. EJ058628.

Barkham, M. (1988). "Empathy in counselling and psychotherapy: Present status and future directions." *Counselling Psychology Quarterly* 1(4): 407–427.

Barkham, M., Firth-Cozens, J., & Shapiro, D. A. (1989). "Change in prescriptive versus exploratory therapy: Older client's responses to therapy." *Counselling Psychology Quarterly* 2(4): 395–403.

Barkham, M., & Shapiro, D. A. (1986). "Counselor verbal response modes and experienced empathy." *Journal of Counseling Psychology* 33(1): 3–10.

Barnabei, F. (1971). "Determining the effects of three counselor verbal responses on client verbal behaviour." ED073386.

Barnes, H. L., & Olsen, D. H. (1985). "Parent–adolescent communication and the circumplex model." *Child Development* 56: 438–447.

Barnett, M. A. (1988). "Reasons for not wanting help." *Journal of Genetic Psychology* 149: 127–129.

Barnett, M. A., McMinimy, V., Flouer, G., & Masbad, I. (1987). "Adolescents' evaluations of peers' motives for helping." *Journal of Youth and Adolescence* 16(6): 579–586.

Barrett, C. L., Hampe, I. E., & Miller, L. C. (1978). "Research on child psychotherapy." In S. L. Garfield & A. E. Bergin (Eds.), *Handbook of Psychotherapy and Behaviour Change: An Empirical Analysis* (2d ed.). New York: Wiley.

Barrett, T. N., & Scott, T. B. (1989). "Development of the grief experience questionnaire." *Suicide and Life Threatening Behaviour* 19(2): 201–215.

Barrett-Lennard, G. T. (1962). "Dimensions of therapist response as causal factors in therapeutic change." *Psychological Monographs* 76 (43).

Baumrind, D. (1978). "Reciprocal rights and responsibilities in parent–child relations." *Journal of Social Issues* 34: 179–196.

Bavidge, N. (1995). "Hurt that has to be heard." *Times Educational Supplement*, November 10.

Bayer, D. L. (1986). "The effects of two methods of affective education on self-concept in seventh grade students." *The School Counselor* 34(2): 123–133.

Beach, A. L. (1970). *Effects of group model reinforcement counseling on behaviour of seventh and eighth grade students.* Ph.D. dissertation, Stanford University.

Bednar, R. L., & Parker, C. A. (1969). *Client susceptibility to persuasion and counseling outcome.* Paper presented at the American Psychological Association convention, Washington, DC. EJ051517.

Beeler, K. J. (1989). "Matching student concerns and modes of counseling intervention." *Journal of College Student Development* 30: 185–186.

Begley, C. E., & Lieberman, L. R. (1970). "Patient expectations of therapist techniques." *Journal of Clinical Psychology* 26: 112–116.

Bekaouche, A. (1974). *A study of the effectiveness of transactional analysis and transactional analysis modified on juvenile delinquents.* Ph.D. dissertation, American University.

Bell, W. J. (1989). "Client perceptions of the effectiveness of divorce and adjustment groups." *Journal of Social Service Research* 13(2): 9–32.

Benbenishty, R., & Schul, Y. (1987). "Client–therapist congruence of expectations over the course of therapy." *British Journal of Clinical Psychology* 26: 17–24.

Benson, R. L., & Blocher, D. H. (1967). "Evaluation of developmental counseling with groups of low achievers in a high school setting." *The School Counselor* 14: 215–220.

Berden, G. F., Althaus, M., & Verhulst, F. C. (1990). "Major life events in the behavioural functioning of children." *Journal of Child Psychology and Psychiatry* 31(6): 949–959.

Bernard, H. S. (1989). "Guidelines to minimise premature terminations." *International Journal of Group Psychotherapy* 39(4): 523–529.

Bernard, H. S., & Drob, S. L. (1989). "Premature termination: A clinical study." *Group* 13(1): 11–22.

Berndt, T. J. (1979). "Developmental conformity to peers and parents." *Developmental Psychology* 18: 372–379.

Berndt, T. J., & Miller, K. E. (1989). "Adolescents' perceptions of friends' and parents' influence on aspects of their school adjustment." *Journal of Early Adolescence* 9(4): 419–435.

Bernstein, B. L., Wade, P., & Hoffman, B. (1987). "Students' race and preferences for counselor's race, sex, age, and experience." *Journal of Multicultural Counseling and Development* 15(2): 60–70.

Bird, G. W., & Harris, R. L. (1990). "A comparison of role strain and coping strategies by gender and family structure among early adolescents." *Journal of Early Adolescence* 10: 141–158.

Bisese, S. E. (1990). "Therapist specific communication styles and patient resistance: An analogue study." *Counseling Psychology Quarterly* 3(2): 171–182.

Bishop, J. B. (1971). "Another look at counselor, client, and supervisor ratings of counselor effectiveness. *Counselor Education and Supervision* 10(4): 319–323. EJ042329.

Blaine, G. B., & McArthur, C. C. (1958). "What happened in therapy as seen by the patient and his psychiatrist." *Journal of Nervous and Mental Disease* 127: 344–350.

Blier, M. J., Atkinson, D. R., & Geer, C. A. (1987). "Effect of client gender and counselor gender and sex roles on willingness to see the counselor." *Journal of Counseling Psychology* 34: 27–30.

Bloom, B. S., & Sosniak, L. A. (1981). "Talent development versus schooling." *Educational Leadership* (92): 86–94.

Blos, P. (1979). *The Adolescent Passage: Developmental Issues.* New York: International Universities Press.

Blum, R., McKay, C., Resnick, M., Geer, L., & Campbell, R. (1989). *The State of Adolescent Health in Minnesota.* Minneapolis: University of Minnesota Press.

Blyth, D. A., Hill, J. P., & Theil, K. S. (1982). "Early adolescents' significant others: Grade and gender differences in perceived relationships with familial and non-familial adults and young people." *Journal of Youth and Adolescence* 11: 425–450.

Bo, I. (1989). "The significant people in the social networks of adolescents." In K. Hurrelmann & U. Engel (Eds.), *The Social World of Adolescents.* Berlin & New York: Walter De Gruyter.

Board, F. A. (1959). "Patients' and physicians' judgements of outcome of psychotherapy in an outpatient clinic." *Archives of General Psychiatry* 1: 185–196.

Bogie, D. W., & Bogie, C. E. (1976). "The counselor–client contact variable and occupational aspiration–expectation discrepancies." *Vocational Guidance Quarterly* 25(1): 50–57. EJ150000.

Boldero, J., & Fallon, B. (1995). "Adolescent help-seeking: What do they get help for and from whom?" *Journal of Adolescence* 18(3): 193–209.

Booth, J. A. (1974). *Client perceptions of prison counselor effectiveness*. Paper presented at the annual meeting of the Canadian Guidance and Counseling Association, Vancouver. ED119094.

Bosworth, K. (1995). "Caring for others and being cared for others." *Phi Delta Kappan* (May): 686–693.

Bowerman, C. E., & Kinch, J. W. (1959). "Changes in family and peer orientation of children between fourth and tenth grades." *Social Forces* 37: 206–211.

Bowlby, J. (1973). "Self-reliance and some conditions that promote it." In R. Gosling (Ed.), *Support, Innovation, and Autonomy*. London: Tavistock Publications.

Boyle, M. H., Offord, D. R., Hofmann, H. G., Catlin, G. P., Byles, J. A., Cadman, D. T., Crawford, J. W., Links, P. S., Rae-Grant, N. I., & Szatmari, P. (1987). "Ontario child health study." *Archives of General Psychiatry* 44: 826–831.

Bozarth, J. D., & Grace, D. P. (1970). "Objective ratings and client perceptions of therapeutic conditions with university counseling center clients." *Journal of Clinical Psychology* 26(1): 117–118. EJ017228.

Bozarth, J. D., & Rubin, S. E. (1975). "Empirical observations of rehabilitation counselor performance and outcome: Some implications." *Rehabilitation Counseling Bulletin* 19(1): 294–298. EJ129032.

Bozer, J. A. (1985). *A Study of Elementary Guidance Counseling*. Knoxville: Bureau of Educational Research and Service, Tennessee University.

Brabham, R. E., & Thoreson, R. W. (1973). "Relationship of client preferences and counselor's physical disability." *Journal of Counseling Psychology* 20(1): 10–15. EJ097662.

Brannen, J., & Collard, J. (1982). *Marriages in Trouble: The Process of Seeking Help*. London: Tavistock Publications.

Branwhite, T. (1988). "The PASS survey: School-based preferences of 500+ adolescent consumers." *Educational Studies* 14(2): 165–176.

———. (1994). "Bullying and student distress: Beneath the tip of the iceberg." *Educational Psychology* 14(1): 59–71.

———. (1996). *Adolescent Problems, Perspectives, and School-Based Helping*. Ph.D. dissertation, University of Hull.

Breakwell, G. M. (1987). "The evaluation of student counselling: A review of the literature." *British Journal of Guidance and Counselling* 15(2): 131–139.

Brehm, S. S., & Brehm, J. W. (1981). *Psychological Reactance: A Theory of Freedom and Control*. New York: Academic Press.

Brischetto, C. M., & Verluzzi, T. V. (1981). "Client perceptions in an initial interview as a function of therapist sex and expertness." *Journal of Clinical Psychology* 37(1): 82–87. EJ241957.

Brittain, C. V. (1963). "Adolescent choices and parent–peer cross-pressures." *American Sociological Review* 28: 385–391.

Brown, J. M., O'Keefe, J., Sanders, S. H., & Baker, B. (1986). "Developmental changes in children's cognition to stressful and painful situations." *Journal of Pediatric Psychology* 11(3): 343–357.

Brown, P., & Manela, R. (1977). "Client satisfaction with marital and divorce counseling." *Family Co-Ordinator* 26(3): 294–302. EJ161988.

Bruyere, D. H. (1975). *The effects of client-centered and behavioural group counseling on classroom behaviour and self-concept of junior high school students who exhibited disruptive classroom behaviour.* Ph.D. dissertation, University of Oregon.

Bryman, A. (1989). *Research Methods and Organisation Studies.* London: Unwin Hyman.

Budman, S. H. (1990). "The myth of termination in brief therapy: Or, it ain't over till it's over." In J. K. Zeig & S. G. Gilligan (Eds.), *Brief Therapy: Myths, Methods, and Metaphors* (pp. 206–220). New York: Brunner-Mazel.

Buhrmester, D., & Furman, W. (1987). "The development of companionship and intimacy." *Child Development* 58: 1101–1113.

Burke, B., & Hampton, G. (1979). "Attitudes of university students and staff to student counselling." *Student Counselling and Research Unit Bulletin* 16: 1–118. Published by the University of New South Wales.

Burke, R. J., & Weir, T. (1979). "Helping responses of parents and peers and adolescent well-being." *Journal of Psychology* 102: 49–62.

Burningham, S. (1994). *Young People under Stress: A Parent's Guide.* London: Virago Press.

Byrne, T. P. (1979). "Differential client satisfaction with Holland's self-directed search." *Journal of College Student Personnel* 20(6): 502–505. EJ217223.

Cairns, E., McWhirter, L., Barry, R., & Duffy, U. (1991). "The development of psychological well-being in late adolescence." *Journal of Child Psychology and Psychiatry* 32(4): 635–643.

Campbell, D. G. (1965). *The Results of Counselling: Twenty-Five Years Later.* Philadelphia: W. B. Saunders.

Caplan, S. W. (1957). "The effect of group counseling on junior high school boys' concepts of themselves in school." *Journal of Counseling Psychology* 4: 124–128.

Capone, T. A. (1980). "Client perceptions of two antagonist programmes." *Journal of Drug Education* 10(1): 63–67. EJ220981.

Carmin, C. A. (1986). "Threat to self-esteem and counselee response to help: An introductory investigation of self-help, help-seeking, and rejection of help behaviours." *Dissertation Abstracts International* A47: 2952.

Carter, S. P., & Janzen, H. L. (1994). "Peer counseling or peer support? There is a difference." *Canadian Journal of School Psychology* 10(1): 36–42.

Carty, L. (1988). *Developmental peer counseling and health promotion.* Paper presented at the 14th annual meeting of the National Consultation on Vocational Counseling, Ottawa. ED302793.

Casey, R. J., & Berman, J. S. (1985). "The outcome of psychotherapy with children." *Psychological Bulletin* 98(2): 388–400.

Caspar, R. C., Belanoff, J., & Offer, D. (1996). "Gender differences, but no racial group differences in self-reported psychiatric symptoms in adolescents." *Journal of the American Academy of Child and Adolescent Psychiatry*.

Central Statistical Office. (1992). *Annual Abstract of Statistics* (no. 128). London: H.M.S.O.

Cervantes, L. F. (1969). *The Dropout: Causes and Cures.* Ann Arbor: University of Michigan Press.

Chambers, A. A. (1989). *Client judgement of therapist characteristics: A factor in treatment.* Paper presented at the annual meeting of the American Psychological Association, New Orleans. ED315712.

Chance, E. (1959). *Families in treatment: From the viewpoint of the patient, the clinician, and the researcher.* New York: Basic Books.

Chartier, G. M., & Lassen, M. K. (1994). "Adolescent depression: Children's depression inventory norms, suicidal ideation, and weak gender effects." *Adolescence* 29(116): 859–873.

Chase, C. I. (1981). "Teenagers are mostly positive about high-school." *Phi Delta Kappan* 62(7): 526.

Chaudhari, U. S. (1976). "Sex and culture differences in life problems and interests of adolescents." *Alberta Journal of Educational Research* 22(1): 88–96.

Chen, A. C., & Treede, R. D. (1985). "The McGill pain questionnaire in the assessment of phasic and tonic experimental pain: Behavioural evaluation of the 'pain inhibiting pain' effect." *Pain* 22(1): 67–79.

Cherbosque, J. (1987). "Differential effects of counselor self-disclosure statements on perception of the counselor and willingness to disclose: A cross-cultural study." *Psychotherapy* 24(3): 434–437.

Cherry, N., & Gear, R. (1987). "Young peoples' perceptions of their vocational guidance needs: 1. Priorities and pre-occupations." *British Journal of Guidance and Counselling* 15(1): 59–71.

Chivian, E., Mack, J. E., Waletzley, J. P., Lazaroff, C., Doctor, R., & Goldenring, J. M. (1985). "Soviet children and the threat of nuclear war: A preliminary study." *American Journal of Orthopsychiatry* 55: 484–502.

Christen, K. C., Birk, J. M., & Sedlacek, W. E. (1975). *Follow-up of clients placed on a counseling center waiting list: Where have they gone?* Anapolis: University of Maryland, Counseling Center Research Report No. 4-75.

Clarke-Stewart, A., & Koch, J. B. (1983). *Children: Development through Adolescence.* New York: Wiley.

Clements, B. E. (1966). "Transitional adolescents, anxiety, and group counseling." *Personnel and Guidance Journal* 45: 67–71.

Cline, V. B., Jackson, S. L., Klein, N., Mejia, J., & Turner, C. (1987). "Marital therapy outcome measured by therapist, client, and behaviour change." *Family Process* 26: 255–267.

Coats, D., Renzaglia, G. J., & Embree, M. C. (1983). "When helping backfires: Help and helplessness." In J. D. Fisher, A. Nadler, & B. M. De Paulo (Eds.), *New Directions in Helping: Volume 1. Recipients' Reactions to Aid.* New York: Academic Press.

Cochran, S. V., & Stamler, V. L. (1989). "Differences between mutual and client-initiated nonmutual terminations in a university counseling center." *Journal of College Student Development* 30(1): 58–61.

Cohen, L. H., Burt, C. E., & Bjork, J. P. (1987). "Life stress and adjustment: Effects of life events experienced by young adolescents and their parents." *Developmental Psychology* 23: 583–592.

Coleman, J. C. (1989). "The focal theory of adolescence: A psychological perspective." In U. Bielefeld (Ed.), *The Social World of Adolescence: International Perspectives*. Berlin: Walter de Gruyter.

Coleman, J. C., & Hendry, L. (1990). *The Nature of Adolescence* (2d ed.). London: Routledge.

Collins, J. K., & Harper, J. F. (1974). "Problems of adolescents in Sydney, Australia." *Journal of Genetic Psychology* 125: 187–194.

Conger, J., & Petersen, A. C. (1984). *Adolescence and Youth: Psychological Development in a Changing World*. New York: Harper & Row.

Conte, H. R., Plutchik, R., Buckley, P., Warren Spence, D., & Karasu, T. B. (1989). "Outpatients view their psychiatric treatment." *Home and Community Psychiatry* 40(6): 641–643.

Cooley, E. J., & Lajoy, R. (1980). "Therapeutic relationship and improvement as perceived by clients and therapists." *Journal of Clinical Psychology* 36(2): 562–570. EJ223107.

Cooper, H. M. (1982). "Scientific guidelines for conducting integrative research reviews." *Review of Educational Research* 52: 291–302.

———. (1989). *Integrating Research: A Guide For Literature Reviews*. Newbury Park, CA: Sage.

Coopersmith, S. (1967). *The Antecedents of Self-Esteem*. San Francisco: W. H. Freeman.

Copeland, E. P., & Hess, R. S. (1995). "Differences in young adolescents' coping strategies based on gender and ethnicity." *Journal of Adolescence* 15(2): 203–219.

Cordell, G. (1973). *The effect of structured group counseling on the self-concept, attendance, and achievement of absentee-prone high school students*. Unpublished Ph.D. dissertation, Ohio State University.

Corn, K. L., & Moore, D. D. (1992). "Reach for the STARS: Students teaching and reaching students: A two-faceted peer facilitating program at Greenfield Central High School." *The School Counselor* 40(1): 68–77.

Cowie, H., & Pecherek, A. (1994). *Counselling: Approaches and Issues in Education*. London: Fulton.

Craig, S. S., & Hennessy, J. J. (1989). "Personality differences and expectations about counseling." *Journal of Counseling Psychology* 36(4): 401–407.

Cramer, D. (1988). "Self-esteem and facilitative close relationships: A cross-lagged panel correlation analysis." *British Journal of Social Psychology* 27: 115–126.

———. (1990a). "Self-esteem and close relationships: A statistical refinement." *British Journal of Social Psychology* 29: 189–191.

———. (1990b). "Towards assessing the therapeutic value of Roger's core conditions." *Counseling Psychology Quarterly* 3(1): 57–66.

———. (1991). "Self-esteem and Roger's core conditions in close friends: A latent variable path analysis of panel data." *Person-Centered Review* (Spring issue).

————. (1994). *Introducing Statistics for Social Research: Step-by-Step Calculations and Computer Techniques Using SPSS*. London: Routledge.

Crane, D. R., Griffith, W., & Hill, R. D. (1986). "Influence of therapist skills on client perceptions of marriage and family therapy outcome: Implications for supervision." *Journal of Marital and Family Therapy* 9(1): 91–96. EJ331031.

Csikszentmihalyi, M., & Larson, R. W. (1984). *Being Adolescent: Conflict and Growth in the Adolescent Years*. New York: Basic Books.

Dadfar, S., & Friedlander, M. L. (1982). "Differential attitudes of international students toward seeking professional psychological help." *Journal of Counseling Psychology* 29(3): 335–338.

Dalton, D. R., & Cosier, R. A. (1989). "Developmental and psychometric properties of the decision conflict and co-operation questionnaire." *Educational and Psychological Measurement* 49(3): 617–700.

Darden, D. W. (1973). *A study of some effects of early change agent behavior on a group client system*. Ph.D. dissertation, Florida State University. ED078288.

Deforest, C., & Stone, G. L. (1980). "Effects of sex and intimacy level on self disclosure." *Journal of Counseling Psychology* 27: 93–96.

Department for Education and Employment. (1994a). *Circular 8/94: Pupil Behaviour and Discipline*. London: Central Office of Information.

Department for Education and Employment. (1994b). *Code of Practice for the Identification and Assessment of Special Educational Needs*. London: Central Office of Information.

De Paulo, B. M. (1978a). "Accepting help from teachers—when the teachers are children." *Human Relations* 31: 459–474.

————. (1978b). "Help-seeking from the recipient's point of view." *JSAS Catalog of Selected Documents in Psychology* 8: 62 (Manuscript No. 1721).

Deschesnes, M. (1994). "Evaluation of a peer-support network after three years of implementation in a secondary school." *Canadian Journal of Community Mental Health* 13(2): 111–126.

De Shazer, S. (1991). *Putting Difference to Work*. New York: W. W. Norton.

De Weerdt, P. A. (1986). "School counsellors perceptual sex role differences in Dutch secondary education: A pilot study." *International Journal for the Advancement of Counseling* 11: 183–195.

Dill-Standiford, T. J., Stiles, W. B., & Rorer, L. G. (1988). "Counselor–client agreement on session impact." *Journal of Counseling Psychology* 35(1): 47–55.

Dolan, B. (1995). "A teen hot-line." *Adolescence* 30(117): 195–200.

Dole, A. (1977). *A penny for your thoughts: Counselor behaviours and client satisfaction as a function of counselor retrospections*. Paper presented at the annual meeting of the American Educational Research Association, San Francisco. ED173737.

Dolliver, R. H. (1986). "Counselor directiveness and client task-readiness reviewed." *The Counseling Psychologist* 14(3): 461–464.

Donnan, H. H., & Mitchell, H. D. (1979). "Preferences for older versus younger counselors among a group of elderly persons." *Journal of Counseling Psychology* 26: 514–518.

Dorhout, A. (1983). "Student and teacher perceptions of preferred teacher behaviours among the academically gifted." *Gifted Child Quarterly* 27: 122–123.

Dorn, F. (1980). *The Client Satisfaction Survey: An Exploration in Self-Evaluation.* Personal Counseling Service, College Station, Texas A&M University. ED204671.

Douvan, E., & Adelson, J. (1966). *The Adolescent Experience.* New York: Wiley.

Dubow, E. F., Lovko, K. R., & Kausch, D. F. (1990). "Demographic differences in health concerns and perceptions of helping agents." *Journal of Clinical Psychology* 19(1): 44–54.

Duckro, P. N., Beal, D., & George, C. E. (1979a). "Effects of failure to meet client preference in a counseling interview analogue." *Journal of Counseling Psychology* 26: 9–14. EJ223005.

———. (1979b). "Research on the effects of disconfirmed client role expectations in psychotherapy: A review." *Psychological Bulletin* 86(2): 260–275.

Dunne, F., & Thompson, A. (1995). "Families' experience of us." *Context* 22: 37–39.

Dupre, R. W. (1970a). *The effects of counselor response upon the premature termination of clients.* Ruston: Louisiana Polytechnic Institute. EDO40447.

———. (1970b). *The effects of group counseling on the self concepts of typical junior high school students* (Research Paper No. 34). Boulder: University of Colorado, Laboratory for Educational Research.

Durlak, J. A., Fuhrman, T., & Lampman, N. (1991). "Effectiveness of cognitive-behavioural therapy for maladapting children: A meta-analysis." *Psychological Bulletin* 110(2): 204–214.

Durrant, M. (1995). *Creative Strategies for School Problems.* New York: W. W. Norton.

Eastman, M., & Rosen, S. C. (1994). *Taming the Dragon in Your Child.* New York: Wiley.

Egan, G. (1990). *The Skilled Helper* (4th ed.). Pacific Grove, CA: Brooks-Cole.

Eisenberg, N. (1983). "Developmental aspects of recipients' reactions to aid." In J. D. Fisher, A. Nadler, & B. M. De Paulo (Eds.), *New Directions in Helping: Volume 1. Recipients' Reactions to Aid.* New York: Academic Press.

Elliott, R. (1979). "How clients perceive helper behaviours." *Journal of Counseling Psychology* 26(4): 285–294. EJ223250.

———. (1980). *Measuring and predicting the effectiveness of helping responses: Correlates of client and counselor perceptions.* Paper presented at the annual meeting of the Society for Psychotherapy Research, Pacific Grove, California. ED192229.

———. (1985). "Helpful and non-helpful events in brief counselling interviews: An empirical taxonomy." *Journal of Counseling Psychology* 32: 307–322.

———. (1986). "Interpersonal process recall (IPR) as a psychotherapy process research method." In L. Greenberg & W. Pinsof (Eds.), *The Psychotherapeutic Process: A Research Handbook.* New York: Guilford.

Eme, R., Maisiak, R., & Goodale, W. (1979). "Seriousness of adolescent problems." *Adolescence* 14: 93–99.

Engen, H. B., Laing, J., & Sawyer, R. (1988). "College-bound students satisfaction with guidance services." *The School Counselor* 36(2): 112–117.

Epperson, D. L., Bushway, D. J., & Warman, R. E. (1983). "Client self-termination after one counseling session: Effects of problem recognition, counselor gender, and counselor experience." *Journal of Counseling Psychology* 30(3): 307–315.

Erikson, E. H. (1959). *Identity and the Life Cycle.* New York: W. W. Norton.

Esser, G., Schmidt, M. H., & Woerner, W. (1990). "Epidemiology and course of psychiatric disorders in school-age children: Results of a longitudinal study." *Journal of Child Psychology and Psychiatry* 31(2): 243–263.

Evans, B. J., Kiellerup, F. D., Stanley, R. O., Burrows, G. D., & Sweet, B. (1987). "A communication skills programme for increasing patients' satisfaction with general practice consultations." *British Journal of Medical Psychology* 60: 373–378.

Evans, G., & Poole, M. (1987). "Adolescent concerns: A classification of life skills areas." *Australian Journal of Education* 31: 55–72.

Ewing, T. N. (1974). "Racial similarity of client and counselor and client satisfaction with counseling." *Journal of Counseling Psychology* 21(5): 446–449. EJ108773.

Falchikov, N. (1986). "Images of adolescence: An investigation into the accuracy of the image of adolescence constructed by British newspapers." *Journal of Adolescence* 9: 167–180.

Feifel, H., & Eells, J. (1963). "Patients and therapists assess the same psychotherapy." *Journal of Consulting Psychology* 27(4): 310–318.

Feldstein, J. C. (1979). "Effects of counselor sex and sex-role and client sex on clients' perceptions and self-disclosure in a counseling analogue study." *Journal of Counseling Psychology* 26(5): 437–443. EJ223299.

Felker, D. W., Stanwyk, D. J., & Kay, R. S. (1973). "The effects of a teacher program in self-concept enhancement on pupils' self-concept and intellectual achievement responsibility." *Journal of Educational Research* 66: 443–445.

Ferguson, G. A., & Takane, Y. (1989). *Statistical Analysis in Psychology and Education.* New York: McGraw-Hill.

Fiester, A. (1974). "Pre-therapy expectations, perception of the initial interview, and early psychotherapy termination: A multivariate study." *Dissertation Abstracts International 35,* 1907B (University Microfilms No. 74-21729).

Finney, B. C., & Van Dalsem, E. (1969). "Group counseling for gifted underachieving high school students." *Journal of Counseling Psychology* 16: 87–97.

Fish, J. M. (1970). "Empathy and the reported emotional experiences of beginning psychotherapists." *Journal of Consulting and Clinical Psychology* 35: 64–69.

Fisher, D. L., & Fraser, B. J. (1983). "A comparison of actual and preferred classroom environments as perceived by science teachers and students." *Journal of Research in Science Teaching* 20: 55–61.

Fisher, J. D. (1983). "Recipient reactions to aid: The parameters of the field." In J. D. Fisher, A. Nadler, & B. M. De Paulo (Eds.), *New Directions in Helping: Volume 1: Recipient Reactions to Aid*. New York: Academic Press.

Fisher, J. D., Nadler, A., & Witcher-Alagna, S. (1983). "Four conceptualisations of reactions to aid." In J. D. Fisher, A. Nadler, & B. M. De Paulo (Eds.), *New Directions in Helping: Volume 1. Recipient Reactions to Aid*. New York: Academic Press.

Fitzgerald, M., Joseph, A. P., Hayes, M., & O'Regan, M. (1995). "Leisure activities of adolescent schoolchildren." *Journal of Adolescence* 18: 349–358.

Fleming, J. E., Offord, D. R., & Boyle, M. H. (1989). "Prevalence of childhood and adolescent depression in the community." *British Journal of Psychiatry* 155: 647–654.

Fontana, D. (1987). "Knowing about being." *Changes* 5(2): 334–347.

———. (1991). *Psychology for Teachers* (2d ed.). London: British Psychological Society, Leicester, with Macmillan.

Foote, M. (1975). "Tolerance of ambiguity: A variable in client and counsellor pairing." *Canadian Counselor* 9(1): 63–67. EJ120684.

Forehand, R., Neighbours, B., & Wierson, M. (1991). "The transition to adolescence: The role of gender and stress in problem behaviour and competence." *Journal of Child Psychology and Psychiatry* 32(6): 929–937.

Frank, J. D. (1961). *Persuasion and Healing*. Baltimore: Johns Hopkins University Press.

Frank, J., Gliedman, L., Imber, S., Nash, E., & Stone, A. (1957). "Why patients leave psychotherapy." *Archives of Neurological Psychiatry* 77: 283–299.

Frankel, K. A. (1990). "Girls' perception of peer relationship support and stress." *Journal of Early Adolescence* 10(1): 69–88.

Freeman, H. R. (1989). "Influence of client and counselor characteristics on satisfaction with counseling services." *Journal of Mental Health Counseling* 11(4): 375–383.

Freud, A. (1950). *Adolescence: Psychoanalytic Study of the Child*. New York: International Universities Press.

Freud, S. (1953). *A General Introduction to Psychoanalysis*. New York: Permabooks.

Freund, R. D., Russell, T. T., & Schweitzer, S. (1991). "Influence of length of delay between intake session and initial counseling session on client perceptions of counselors and counseling outcomes." *Journal of Counseling Psychology* 38(1): 3–8.

Friedenberg, E. (1959). *The Vanishing Adolescent*. Boston: Beacon.

Friedland, B. V. (1972). *Changes in problems of 9th grade students as an outcome of Adlerian counseling*. Ph.D. dissertation, West Virginia University.

Friedman, A. S., Glickman, N. W., & Kovach, J. A. (1986). "Comparisons of perceptions of the environments of adolescent drug treatment residential and outpatient programs by staff versus clients and by sex of staff and clients." *American Journal of Drug and Alchohol Abuse* 12(1&2): 31–52.

Friedman, I. A. (1991). "Areas of concern and sources of advice for Israeli adolescents." *Adolescence* 26(104): 967–976.

Frisz, R. H., & Lane, J. R. (1987). "Student user evaluations of peer advisor services." *Journal of College Student Personnel* (May): 241–245.

Frydenberg, E., & Lewis, R. (1993). "Boys play sport and girls turn to others: Age, gender, and ethnicity as determinants of coping." *Journal of Adolescence* 16: 253–266.

Fukuhara, M. (1986). "The attitude of students towards consultation and counselling." *School Psychology International* 7(2): 76–82.

Fuller, F., & Hill, C. E. (1985). "Counselor and helpee perceptions of counselor intentions in relation to outcome in a single counseling session." *Journal of Counseling Psychology* 32(3): 329–338.

Furman, W., & Buhrmester, D. (1985). "Children's perceptions of the personal relationships in their social networks." *Developmental Psychology* 21(6): 1016–1024.

Further Education Funding Council/Office for Standards in Education. (1994). *16–19 Guidance.* London: Central Office of Information.

Galassi, J. P., Crace, R. K., Martin, G. A., James, R. M., & Wallace, R. L. (1992). "Client preferences and anticipations in career counseling: A preliminary investigation." *Journal of Counseling Psychology* 39(1): 46–55.

Galbo, J. J. (1980). "Adolescent alienation in secondary schools: A review of the literature." *The High School Journal* 64(1): 26–31.

———. (1983). "Adolescents' perceptions of significant adults." *Adolescence* 18(70): 417–427.

———. (1986). "Adolescents' perceptions of significant adults: Implications for the family, the school and youth serving agencies." *Children and Youth Services Review* 8: 37–51.

———. (1988). "An exploration of the effects of the relationships of adolescents and adults on learning in secondary schools." *The High School Journal* (December–January): 97–102.

———. (1989). "The teacher as significant adult: A review of the literature." *Adolescence* 24(95): 449–555.

———. (1994). "Teachers of adolescents as significant adults and the social construction of knowledge." *The High School Journal* 78(1): 40–44.

Galbo, J. J., Demetrulius, D. M., & Crippen, C. M. (1990). "Recollections of significant adults by pre-service teachers and non-teaching students." *Teacher Education Quarterly* (Spring): 17–39.

Gallagher, M., Millar, R., Hargie, O., & Ellis, R. (1992). "The personal and social worries of adolescents in Northern Ireland: Results of a survey." *British Journal of Guidance and Counselling* 20(3): 274–290.

Gardner, R., & Martin, D. (1989). "The PALS program: A peer counseling program for the junior high school." *Elementary School Guidance and Counseling* 24(1): 68–76.

Garfield, S. L. (1978). "Research on client variables in psychotherapy." In S. L. Garfield & A. E. Bergin (Eds.), *Handbook of Psychotherapy and Behaviour Change* (pp. 192–232). New York: Wiley.

Garmezy, N., & Rutter, R. (1985). "Acute reactions to stress." In R. Rutter & L. Hersov (Eds.), *Child and Adolescent Psychiatry: Modern Approaches*. Oxford: Blackwell Scientific Publications.

Garrison, K. C., & Cunningham, B. W. (1952). "Personal problems of ninth grade pupils." *School Review* 60: 30–33.

Gaskell, G., Wright, D., & O'Miurcheartaigh, C. (1993). "Reliability of surveys." *The Psychologist* 6(11): 500–502.

Gavin, L. A., & Furman, W. (1989). "Age differences in adolescents' perceptions of their peer group." *Developmental Psychology* 25: 827–834.

Gearhart, W. R., Gentilcore, E., Rhinehart, B. R., Simon, W. E., & Simon, M. G. (1977). "Effects of Syosset's developmental learning program on self-concept: Some preliminary data." *Perceptual and Motor Skills* 44(2): 445–446.

Gelso, C. J. (1973). "Effect of audio-recording and video-recording on client satisfaction and self-expression." *Journal of Consulting and Clinical Psychology* 40(3): 455–461. EJ481087.

Gelso, C. J., Brooks, L., & Karl, N. J. (1975). "Perceptions of counselors and other helpers: A consumer analysis." *Journal of College Student Personnel* 16: 287–292.

Gelso, C. J., & Carter, J. A. (1994). "Components of the psychotherapy relationship: Their interaction and unfolding during treatment." *Journal of Counseling Psychology* 41(3): 296–306.

Gelso, C. J., & Karl, N. J. (1974). "Perceptions of counselors and help-givers: What's in a label?" *Journal of Counseling Psychology* 21(3): 243–247.

Getsinger, S. H., & Garfield, N. J. (1976). "Male students' perceptions of counselors, guidance counselors, and counseling psychologists." *Journal of College Student Personnel* 17: 7–10.

Getz, H. G., & Miles, J. H. (1978). "Women and peers as counselors: A look at client preferences." *Journal of College Student Personnel* 19(1): 37–40. EJ175397.

Gibbons, J. S., Bow, I., Butler, J., & Powell, J. (1979). "Clients' reaction to task-centred casework." *British Journal of Social Work* 9(2): 201–215.

Giller, V. L., Dial, J. G., & Chan, F. (1986). "The street survival skills questionnaire: A correlational study." *American Journal of Mental Deficiency* 91(1): 67–71.

Gillies, P. (1989). "A longitudinal study of the hopes and worries of adolescents." *Journal of Adolescence* 12: 69–81.

Gilliland, B. E. (1968). "Small group counseling with Negro adolescents in a public high school." *Journal of Counseling Psychology* 15: 147–152.

Godwin, T. C., & Crouch, J. G. (1989). "Subjects' religious orientation, counselor's orientation and skill, and expectations for counseling." *Journal of Psychology and Theology* 17(3): 284–292.

Goldberg, D., & Huxley, P. (1988). *Mental Illness in the Community: The Pathway to Psychiatric Care*. London: Tavistock Publications.

Goldberg, S., Lacombe, S., Levinson, D., Parker, K. R., Ross, C., & Sommers, F. (1985). "Thinking about the threat of nuclear war: Relevance to mental health." *American Journal of Orthopsychiatry* 55: 503–511.

Goldenring, J. M., & Doctor, R. (1986). "Teenage worry about nuclear war: North American and European questionnaire studies." *International Journal of Mental Health* 15: 72–92.

Goldstein, A. P. (1962a). *Therapist–Patient Expectancies in Psychotherapy.* New York: Macmillan.

———. (1962b). "Therapist and client expectation of personality change in psychotherapy." *Journal of Counseling Psychology* 7: 180–184.

———. (1981). "Evaluating expectancy effects in cross-cultural counseling and psychotherapy." In A. J. Marsella & P. B. Pedersen (Eds.), *Cross-Cultural Counseling and Psychotherapy.* Elmsford, New York: Pergamon.

Golombek, H., Marton, P., Stein, R., & Korenblum, M. (1987). "Personality functioning status during early and middle adolescence." *Adolescent Psychiatry* 14: 365–377.

Goodman, N. (1969). "Adolescent norms and behaviors: Organisation and conformity." *Merrill-Palmer Quarterly* 15: 199–211.

Goodman, S. H., Sewell, D. R., & Jampol, R. C. (1984). "On going to the counselor: Contributions of life stress and social supports to the decision to seek psychological counseling." *Journal of Counseling Psychology* 31: 306–313

Goodyer, I. M., Wright, C., & Altham, P. (1990). "Recent achievements and adversities in anxious and depressed school-age children." *Journal of Child Psychology and Psychiatry* 31(7): 1063–1077.

Gordon, J., & Grant, G. (1997). *How We Feel.* London: Jessica Kingsley Publishers.

Gordon, M., & Grantham, R. J. (1979). "Helper preference in disadvantaged students." *Journal of Counseling Psychology* 26: 337–343.

Gottman, J. M. (1983). "How children become friends." *Monographs for the Society for Research in Child Development* 48 (3, Serial No. 201).

Gould, E., & Glick, I. D. (1976). "Patient–staff judgements of treatment program helpfulness on a psychiatric ward." *British Journal of Medical Psychology* 49: 23–33.

Gove, W. R., & Herb, T. R. (1974). "Stress and mental illness among the young: A comparison of the sexes." *Social Forces* 53: 256–264.

Graham, P., & Rutter, M. (1973). "Psychiatric disorder in the young adolescent: A follow-up study." *Proceedings of the Royal Society of Medicine* 66: 58–61.

Grantham, R. J., & Gordon, M. E. (1986). "The nature of preference." *Journal of Counseling and Development* 64: 396–400.

Gray, J. (1980). "Guidance in Scottish secondary schools: A client evaluation." *British Journal of Guidance and Counselling* 8(2): 129–145.

Green, R. J., & Herget, M. (1991). "Outcomes of systemic/strategic team consultation: III The importance of therapist warmth and active structuring." *Family Process* 30: 321–336.

Greenberg, L. S. (1986). "Change process research." *Journal of Consulting and Clinical Psychology* 54: 4–9.

Greenberg, M., Seigal, J. M., & Leitch, C. J. (1993). "The nature and importance of attachment relationships to parents and peers during adolescence." *Journal of Youth and Adolescence* 12: 373–386.

Greenberg, M., & Westcott, D. R. (1983). "Indebtedness as a mediator of reactions to aid." In J. D. Fisher, A. Nadler, & B. M. De Paulo (Eds.), *New Directions in Helping: Volume 1. Recipient Reactions to Aid.* San Diego, CA: Academic Press.

Greene, A. L. (1988). "Early adolescents' perceptions of stress." *Journal of Early Adolescence* 8: 391–403.

Greenfield, T. K. (1984). "The role of client satisfaction in evaluating university counseling services." *Evaluation and Program Planning* 6: 315–327.

Greenfield, T. K., & Atkisson, C. C. (1989). "Steps towards a multi-factorial satisfaction scale for primary care and mental health services." *Evaluation and Program Planning* 12: 271–278.

Greenley, J. R., & Mechanic, D. (1976). "Patterns of seeking care for psychological problems. In D. Mechanic (Ed.), *The Growth of Bureaucratic Medicine.* New York: Wiley.

Griffiths, M. (1997). "Friendship and social development in children and adolescents: The impact of electronic technology." *Educational & Child Psychology* 14(3): 25–37.

Grinker, R. R., & Werble, B. (1974). "Mentally healthy young men: Fourteen years later." *Archives of General Psychiatry* 30: 701–704.

Gross, A. E., Fisher, J. D., Nadler, A., Siglitz, E., & Craig, C. (1979). "Initiating contact with a women's counseling service: Some correlates of help utilisation." *Journal of Community Psychology* 7: 42–49.

Gunzburger, D. W. (1985). "Factors related to premature termination of counseling relationships." *Journal of College Student Personnel* 26(5): 456–460. EJ323262.

Gurman, A. S. (1977). "The patients' perception of the therapeutic relationship." In A. S. Gurman & A. M. Razin (Eds.), *Effective Psychotherapy: A Handbook of Research* (pp. 503–543). New York: Pergamon.

Gurney, P. W. (1981). "Using behaviour modification to enhance self-esteem in maladjusted boys." In K. Wheldall (Ed.), *The Behaviourist in the Classroom: Aspects of Applied Behaviour Analysis in British Educational Contexts.* Birmingham: Educational Review Offset Publications.

Gustafson, J. A., & Pennscott, W. W. (1969). "Evaluation of counseling experience by terminated clients." ED039588.

Hagborg, W. J., & Konigsberg, B. (1991). "Multiple perspectives of therapeutic change and the severely emotionally disturbed adolescent." *Psychotherapy* 28(2): 292–297.

Hall, G. S. (1904). *Adolescence: Its Psychology and Its Relations to Physiology, Anthropology, Sociology, Sex, Crime, Religion, and Education* (Volume 1). New York: D. Appleton.

Hamburg, B. A., & Varenhorst, B. B. (1972). "Peer counseling in the secondary schools: A community mental health project for youth." *American Journal of Orthopsychiatry* 42(4): 566–581.

Hannon, D., Breen, R., Murray, B., Watson, D., Hardiman, N., & O'Higgins, K. (1983). *Schooling and sex roles: Sex differences in subject provision and student choice in Irish post-primary schools* (Paper No. 113). Dublin: The Economic and Social Research Institute.

Hardin, S. I., & Yanico, B. (1983). "Counselor gender, type of problem, and expectations about counseling." *Journal of Counseling Psychology* 30: 294–297.

Hardin, S. J., Subich, L. M., & Holvey, J. M. (1988). "Expectancies for counseling in relation to premature termination." *Journal of Counseling Psychology* 35(1): 37–40. EJ369917.

Harman, J. I. (1986). "Relations among components of the empathic process." *Journal of Counseling Psychology* 33(4): 371–376.

Harris, M. B., & Trujillo, A. E. (1975). "Improving study habits of junior high school students through self-management vs. group discussion." *Journal of Counseling Psychology* 22: 513–517.

Harrison, D. K. (1973). *Race as a counselor–client variable in counseling and psychotherapy*. Paper presented at the annual convention of the Association of Black Psychologists, Detroit. ED083488.

Harter, S. (1989). "Causes, correlates, and the functional role of global self-worth: A life-span perspective." In J. Kolligan & R. Sternberg (Eds.), *Perceptions of Competence and Incompetence across the Life-Span*. New Haven, CT: Yale University Press.

Harvey, O. J., Hunt, D. E., & Schroder, H. M. (1961). *Conceptual Systems and Personality Organisation*. New York: Wiley.

Haskins, D.L.B. (1972). *Desensitization of test anxiety in junior high school students*. Ph.D. dissertation, Colorado State University.

Hastin-Bennett, A. M. (1993). *Pears Medical Encyclopedia*. London: Warner Books.

Haughey, J., & Bowman, J. (1980). *Counselling and Guidance Services in Selected Junior High Schools: Utilisation and Identified Need*. Winnipeg: Manitoba Department of Education, Planning and Resources Branch.

Havinghurst, R. (1952). *Developmental Tasks and Education*. New York: McKay.

Hawk, R. (1972). *Four approaches to drug abuse education: An investigation of high school counselors ability to withhold reinforcement in behavioural counseling*. Ph.D. dissertation, Pennsylvania State University.

Hayes, T. J., & Tinsley, H.E.A. (1989). "Identification of latent dimensions of instruments that measure perceptions of and expectations about counseling." *Journal of Counseling Psychology* 36(4): 492–500.

Hayslip, B., & Schneider, L. J. (1985). "Effects of counselor–client age similarity and presenting problem intimacy on client satisfaction." Paper presented at the thirty-first annual convention of the Southwestern Psychological Association, Austin, Texas. ED259254.

Hector, M. A., & Fray, J. S. (1987). "The counseling process, client expectation, and cultural influences: A review." *International Journal for the Advancement of Counseling* 10(4): 237–247.

Heilbrun, A. B. (1970). "Towards resolution of the dependency: Premature termination paradox for females in psychotherapy." *Journal of Consulting and Clinical Psychology* 34(3): 382–385.

———. (1972). "Effects of briefing upon client satisfaction with the initial counseling contact." *Journal of Consulting and Clinical Psychology* 38(1): 50–56. EJ057424.

————. (1974). "Interviewer style, client satisfaction, and premature termination following the initial counseling contact." *Journal of Counseling Psychology* 21(5): 346–350. EJ108753.

Hein, V. A. (1969). *A study of group counseling with selected high school freshmen.* Ph.D. dissertation, Northwestern University.

Heine, R. W. (1953). "A comparison of patients reports on psychotherapeutic experience with psychoanalytic, non-directive, and Adlerian counselors." *American Journal of Psychotherapy* 7: 16–23.

Helms, J. E. (1979). "Perceptions of a sex-fair counselor and her client." *Journal of Counseling Psychology* 26(6): 504–513. EJ223436.

Helwig, A. A. (1982). "Measuring counseling effectiveness: The role of the client." *Journal of Employment Counseling* 19(1): 10–28. EJ261161.

Hendriksen, E. M. (1991). "A peer-helping program in a middle school." *Canadian Journal of Counseling* 25(1); 12–18.

Hendry, L. B., Roberts, W., & Glendinning, A. (1992). "Adolescents' perceptions of significant individuals in their lives." *Journal of Adolescence* 15(3): 255–270.

Heppner, P., & Heesacker, M. (1983). "Perceived counselor characteristics, client expectations, and client satisfaction with counseling." *Journal of Counseling Psychology* 30(1): 31–39.

Herbert, M. (1989). *Discipline: A Positive Guide for Parents.* Oxford: Blackwell.

————. (1994). *Clinical Child Psychology: Social Learning, Development, and Behaviour.* Chichester: Wiley.

Herriott, R. E. (1963). "'Some determinants of educational aspiration." *Harvard Educational Review* 33: 157–177.

Hervey, E. P. (1970). *Comparison of three and six-weeks of group model–reinforcement counseling for improving study habits and attitudes of junior high school students.* Ph.D. dissertation, University of Wisconsin.

Highlen, P. S., & Russell, B. (1980). "Effects of counselor and client sex role on female's counselor preference." *Journal of Counseling Psychology* 27: 157–165.

Hilgard, E. R., & Atkinson, R. C. (1967). *Introduction to Psychology* (4th ed.). New York: Harcourt, Brace & World.

Hill, C. E., Carter, J. A., & O'Farrell, M. K. (1983). "A case-study of the process and outcome of time-limited counseling." *Journal of Counseling Psychology* 30: 3–18.

Hill, C. E., Mahalick, J. R., & Thompson, B. J. (1989). "Therapist self-disclosure." *Psychotherapy* 26: 290–295.

Hill, P. (1993). "Recent advances in selected aspects of adolescent development." *Journal of Child Psychology and Psychiatry* 34(1): 69–99.

H. M. Government. (1989). *The Children Act 1989.* London: H.M.S.O.

Hoffman, M. A., Spokane, A. R., & Magoon, T. M. (1981). "Effects of feedback mode on counselling outcomes using the Strong–Campbell Interest Inventory: Does the counselor really matter?" *Journal of Counseling Psychology* 28(2): 119–125. EJ243575.

Hoinville, G., & Jowell, R. (1978). *Survey Research Practice.* London: Heinemann.

Holland, A., & Thomas, A. (1994). "The relationship of self-esteem to selected personal and environmental resources of adolescents." *Adolescence* 29(114): 345–360.

Hollander-Goldfein, B., & Fosshage, J. L. (1989). "Determinants of patients' choice of therapist." *Psychotherapy* 26(4): 448–461.

Homan, R., & Youngman, J. (1982). "School and church as agencies of religious socialisation." *British Journal of Religious Education* 5: 22–27.

Hooper, D. (1976). "Yesterday's counsellors for tomorrow's problems?" *Marriage Guidance* 16(5): 147–153.

Hooper, R. (1978). "Pupil perceptions of counseling: A response to Murgatroyd." *British Journal of Guidance and Counselling* 6(2): 198–203.

Horenstein, D., & Houston, B. K. (1976). "The expectation–reality discrepancy and premature termination from psychotherapy." *Journal of Clinical Psychology* 32(2): 373–378. EJ147475.

Hortacsu, N. (1989). "Targets of communication during adolescence." *Journal of Adolescence* 12: 253–263.

Howard, K. I., & Orlinsky, D. E. (1972). "Psychotherapeutic processes." *Annual Review of Psychology* 23: 615–668.

Hunt, P. (1985). *Clients' Responses to Marriage Counselling*. Rugby, England: The National Marriage Guidance Council.

Hunter, F. T. (1985). "Adolescents' perceptions of discussions with parents and friends." *Developmental Psychology* 21: 433–440.

Hunter, F. T., & Youniss, J. (1982). "Changes in functions of three relations during adolescence." *Developmental Psychology* 18: 806–811.

Hutchinson, R. L. (1987). *Effects of counselor re-assignments and re-assignment procedures on client anxiety*. Paper presented at the annual meeting of the Midwestern Psychological Association, Chicago. ED291983.

———. (1988). "Effects of counselor re-assignments and re-assignment procedures on client anxiety." *Journal of College Student Development* 29(5): 423–432. EJ383566.

Hutchinson, R. L., & Bottorff, R. L. (1986). "Selected high school counselling services: Student evaluation." *The School Counselor* 33(5): 350–354.

Hutchinson, R. L., & Reagan, C. A. (1989). "Problems for which seniors would seek help from school counselors." *The School Counselor* 36(4): 271–279.

Hutter, A. (1938). "Endegene ein functionelle psychosen bei kindern in den pubertatsjahren." *Archives der Kinderpsychiatrie* 5: 97–102.

Hyatt-Williams, C. (1975). "Puberty and the phases of adolescence." In S. Meyerton (Ed.), *Adolescence and the Crisis of Adjustment*. London: George Allen & Unwin.

Hyman, J. R. (1973). *Systematic desensitization of mathematics anxiety in high school students: The role of mediating responses, imagery, emotionality, and expectancy*. Ph.D. dissertation, Wayne State University.

Institute of Medicine. (1989). *Research on children and adolescents with mental, behavioral, and developmental disorders*. Washington, DC: National Academy Press.

Irving, B., & Parker-Jenkins, M. (1995). "Pupil empowerment: Pupil power?" *Pastoral Care* 13(2): 3–6.

Jackson, G. B. (1980). "Methods for integrative reviews." *Review of Educational Research* 50(3): 438–460.

Johnson, J. J., Rasbury, W. C., & Seigel, L. J. (1986). *Approaches to Child Treatment: Introduction to Theory, Research, and Practice.* New York: Pergamon.

Johnson, R. D. (1990). "Examination of the construct validity of the Expectations About Counseling questionnaire: Brief form for rural counseling applicants." *Dissertation Abstracts International* 51, 1189B (University Microfilms No. 90-12, 572).

Jones, E. E., & Nisbett, R. (1971). "The actor and the observer: Divergent perceptions in the causes of behaviour." In E. E. Jones, D. E. Kanouse, H. H. Kelley, R. E. Nisbett, S. Valens, & B. Weiner (Eds.), *Attribution: Perceiving the Causes of Behaviour.* Morristown, NJ: General Learning Press.

Jones, E. E., Wynne, M. F., & Watson, D. D. (1986). "Client perception of treatment in crisis intervention and longer-term psychotherapies." *Psychotherapy* 23(1): 120–132.

Jones, E. E., & Zoppel, C. L. (1982). "Impact of client and therapist gender on psychotherapy process and outcome." *Journal of Consulting and Clinical Psychology* 50(2): 259–272.

Jorgensen, G. Q., & Rushlau, P. J. (1966). "Interpersonal relationships: A review." Salt Lake City: Utah Studies in Vocational Rehabilitation, Regional Rehabilitation Research Unit, Utah University. ED012083.

Ju, J. J., & Thomas, K. R. (1987). "The accuracy of counselor perceptions of client work values and client satisfaction." *Rehabilitation Counseling Bulletin* 30(3): 157–166.

Juhasz, A. M. (1985). "Measuring self-esteem in early adolescents." *Adolescence* 20(80): 877–887.

June, L. N., & Smith, E. J. (1983). "A comparison of client and counselor expectancies regarding the duration of counseling." *Journal of Counseling Psychology* 30: 596–599.

Kandel, D. B., & Lesser, G. S. (1969a). "Parental and peer influences on educational plans of adolescents." *American Sociological Review* 34: 213–223.

———. (1969b). "Parent–adolescent relationships and independence in the United States and Denmark." *Journal of Marriage and the Family* 31: 348–358.

Kaplan, H. B. (1980). *Deviant Behaviour in Defense of Self.* New York: Academic Press.

Karabenick, S. A., & Knapp, J. R. (1991). "The relationship of academic help-seeking to the use of learning strategies and other instrumental help-seeking in college students." *Journal of Educational Psychology* 83(2): 221–230.

Karpowitz, D. H., & Gurri, I. M. (1979). *Therapy outcome: The influence of the sex of the participants.* Paper presented at the annual convention of the Rocky Mountain Psychological Association, Las Vegas. ED178850.

Kaschak, E. (1978). "Therapist and client: Two views of process and outcome of psychotherapy." *Professional Psychology* (May): 271–277.

Kashani, J. H., Beck, N. C., Hoeper, E. W., Fallahi, C., Corcoran, C. M., McAllister, J. A., Rosenberg, T. K., & Reid, J. C. (1986). "Psychiatric disorders in a community sample of adolescents." *American Journal of Psychiatry* 144(5): 584–589.

Kayser-Boyd, N., Adelman, H. S., & Taylor, L. (1985). "Minor's ability to identify risks and benefits of therapy." *Professional Psychology: Research and Practice* 16(3): 411–417.

Kazmark, P., Greenfield, T., & Cross, H. (1983). "The relationship between level of adjustment and expectations for therapy." *Journal of Clinical Psychology* 39(6): 930–932.

Keats, J. A., Keats, D. M., Biddle, B. J., Bank, B. J., Hauge, R., Wan-Rafaei, M., & Valentin, S. (1983). "Parents, friends, siblings, and adults: Unfolding referent and other important data for adolescents." *International Journal of Psychology* 18: 239–262.

Kelly, H. H. (1967). "Attribution theory in social psychology." In D. Levine (Ed.), *Nebraska Symposium on Motivation* (Volume 15). Lincoln: University of Nebraska Press.

Kelly, K. R., Smith-Hall, A., & Miller, K. L. (1989). "Relation of counselor intention and anxiety to brief counseling outcome." *Journal of Counseling Psychology* 36(2): 158–162.

Keys, W., & Fernandes, C. (1992). *What Do Students Think about School?* Slough, England: National Foundation For Educational Research.

Kidd, J., & Marteau, T. (1992). *Factors affecting patients and doctors' satisfaction.* Paper presented to the Health Psychology Section at the annual conference of the British Psychological Society.

Kim, S., McCleod, J. H., Rader, D., & Johnson, G. (1992). "An evaluation of a prototype school-based peer-counseling program." *Journal of Drug Education* 22(1): 37–53.

Kinnear, P., & Gray, C. (1994). *SPSS for Windows Made Simple.* Hove, Sussex: Erlbaum Associates.

Kissel, S. (1974). "Mothers and therapists evaluate long-term and short-term child therapy." *Journal of Clinical Psychology* 30: 296–298.

Kitwood, T. (1980). *Disclosures to a Stranger: Adolescent Values in an Advanced Industrial Society.* London: Routledge & Kegan Paul.

Kline, F., Adrian, A., & Spevak, M. (1974). "Patients evaluate therapists." *Archives of General Psychiatry* 31: 113–116.

Kobak, R. R., & Sceery, A. (1988). "Attachment in late adolescence: Working models, affect regulation, and representation of self and others." *Child Development* 59: 135–146.

Kofta, M., & Sedek, K. (1989). "Egotism versus generalisation of uncontrollability explanations of helplessness: Reply to Snyder and Frankel." *Journal of Experimental Psychology General* 118(4): 413–416.

Kokotovic, A. M., & Tracey, T. J. (1987). "Premature termination at a university counseling center." *Journal of Counseling Psychology* 34(1): 80–82. EJ409902.

———. (1990). "Working alliance in the early phase of counseling." *Journal of Counseling Psychology* 37(1): 16–21. EJ409902.

Kon, I. S., & Losenkov, V. A. (1978). "Friendship in adolescence: Values and behaviour." *Journal of Marriage and the Family* 40: 143–155.

Kopel, S., & Arkowitz, H. (1975). "The role of attribution and self-perception in behavior change: Implications for behaviour therapy." *Genetic Psychology Monographs* 92: 175–212.

Korsch, B. M., & Negrete, V. F. (1972). "Doctor–patient communication." *Scientific American* 227(2): 66–74.

Kotsopoulos, S., Elwood, S., & Oke, L. (1989). "Parent satisfaction in a child psychiatric service." *Canadian Journal of Psychiatry* 34: 530–533.

Kraft, L. W., & Vraa, C. M. (1975). "Sex composition of groups and patterns of self-disclosure by high-school females." *Psychological Reports* 37: 733–734.

Kretschmer, E. (1951). *Koperbund und Character.* New York: Springer-Verlag.

Krupat, E. (1990). "Physicians and patients: A delicate imbalance." *Psychology Today* 20(11): 22–26.

Kunin, C. C., & Rodin, M. J. (1982). "The interactive effects of counselor gender, physical attractiveness, and status on client self-disclosure." *Journal of Clinical Psychology* 38(1): 84–90.

Kurdek, L. A. (1987). "Gender differences in the psychological symptomatology and coping strategies of young adolescents." *Journal of Early Adolescence* 7(4): 395–410.

L'Abate, L., & McHenry, S. (1983). *Handbook of Marital Interventions.* New York: Grune & Stratton.

La Fountain, R., & Geoffroy, K. (1990). "The efficacy of parent counseling and support groups on the stress levels, self-esteem, and degree of coping of parents of developmentally delayed or handicapped children who are involved in an infant intervention program." ED317896.

Laframboise, T., Dauphinais, P., & Rowe, W. (1978). *A survey of Indian students' perceptions of the counselling experience.* Paper presented at the annual meeting of the American Educational Research Association, Toronto. ED156389.

La Gaipa, J. J. (1979). "A developmental study of the meaning of friendship in adolescence." *Journal of Adolescence* 2: 201–213.

Langner, T. S., & Micheal, S. T. (1963). *Life Stress and Mental Health.* London: The Free Press.

Larson, R., & Lampman-Petraitis, C. L. (1989). "Daily emotional states as reported by children and adolescents." *Child Development* 60: 1250–1260.

Larson, R., & Richards, M. H. (1991). "Daily companionship in late childhood and early adolescence: Changing developmental contexts." *Child Development* 62: 284–300.

Larsson, B. S. (1991). "Somatic complaints and their relationship to depressive symptoms in Swedish adolescents." *Journal of Child Psychology and Psychiatry* 32(5): 821–832.

Lasky, R. G., & Salomone, P. R. (1977). "Attraction to psychotherapy: Influences of therapist status and therapist–patient age similarity." *Journal of Clinical Psychology* 33(2): 511–516.

Lavoie, J. C. (1994). "Identity in adolescence: Issues of theory, structure, and transition." *Journal of Youth and Adolescence* 17: 17–28.

Lawson, G. (1982). "Relation of counsellor traits to evaluation of the counselling relationship by alcoholics." *Journal of Studies on Alcohol* 43(7): 834–839.

Laxer, R. M., Quarter, J., Kooman, A., & Walker, K. (1969). "Systematic desensitisation and relaxation of high test-anxious secondary school students." *Journal of Counseling Psychology* 16: 446.

Lazare, A., Eisenthal, S., & Wasserman, L. (1975). "The customer approach to patient-hood." *Archives of General Psychiatry* 32: 553–558.

Lebow, J. L. (1984). "Research assessing consumer satisfaction with mental health treatment: A review of findings." *Evaluation and Program Planning* 6: 211–236.

Lehmanowsky, M. B. (1991). "Using counselor skills to effectively serve students." *The School Counselor* 38(5): 385–392.

Lennard, H., & Bernstein, A. (1960). *The Anatomy of Psychotherapy*. New York: Columbia University Press.

Leonard, W. P., & Warren, S. J. (1974). "Media services: Client satisfaction as a barometer." *Audio–Visual Instruction* 19(7): 5–6. EJ104570.

Lepper, M. R., Ross, L., & Lau, R. L. (1986). "Persistence of inaccurate beliefs about the self: Perseverence effects in the classroom." *Journal of Personality and Social Psychology* 50(3): 482–491.

Leroux, J. A. (1986). *Sex differences influencing gifted adolescents: An ethnographic study*. Paper presented at the seventieth annual meeting of the American Educational Research Association, San Francisco. ED271934.

Leviton, H. S. (1977). "Consumer feedback on a secondary school guidance program." *Personnel and Guidance Journal* 55: 242–244.

Lewis, C. (1981). "How adolescents approach decisions: Changes over grades seven to twelve and policy implications." *Child Development* 52: 538–544.

Lewis, K. N., Epperson, D. L., & Foley, J. (1989). "Informed entry into counseling: Client's perceptions and preferences resulting from different types and amounts of pre-therapy information." *Journal of Counseling Psychology* 36(3): 279–285.

Lewis, K. N., & Walsh, W. B. (1980). "Effects of value communication style and similarity of values on counselor evaluation." *Journal of Counseling Psychology* 27: 305–314.

Lewis, O. (1993). "Adolescence, social development, and psychotherapy." *American Journal of Psychotherapy* 47(3): 344–352.

Lipkin, S. (1948). "The client evaluates non-directive psychotherapy." *Journal of Consulting Psychology* 12: 137–146.

Littrell, J. M., Malia, J. A., & Vanderwood, M. (1995). "Single-session brief therapy in a high school." *Journal of Counseling and Development* 73: 451–458.

Llewelyn, S. P. (1984). *The experience of patients and therapists in psychological therapy*. Unpublished Ph.D. dissertation, University of Sheffield.

———. (1988). "Psychological therapy as viewed by clients and therapists." *British Journal of Clinical Psychology* 27: 223–237.

Llewelyn, S. P., & Hume, W. I. (1979). "The patients' view of therapy." *British Journal of Medical Psychology* 52: 29–35.

Lonborg, S. D., Daniels, J. A., Houghtonwenger, B., & Brace, L. J. (1991). "Counselor and client verbal response-mode changes during initial counseling sessions." *Journal of Counseling Psychology* 38(4): 394–400.

London, M. (1982). "How do you say good-bye after you've said hello?" *Personnel and Guidance Journal* 60(7): 412–414.

Lorr, M. (1965). "Client perceptions of therapists; A study of the therapeutic relationship." *Journal of Counseling Psychology* 29(2): 146–149.

Losee, N., Auerbach, S. M., & Parham, I. (1988). "Effectiveness of a peer–counselor hotline for the elderly." *Journal of Community Psychology* 16(4): 428–436.

Losier, F., & Ouellette, J. G. (1989). "Perceptions d'etudients universitaires face a un service d'entraide." *Canadian Journal of Counselling Psychology* 23(1): 29–39.

Luborsky, L., McClellan, T., Woody, G. E., O'Brien, C. P., & Auerbach, A. (1985). "Therapist success and its determinants." *Archives of General Psychiatry* 42(6): 602–611.

Luborsky, L., Mintz, J., Auerbach, A., Christoph, P., Bachrach, H., Todd, T., Johnson, M., Cohen, M., & O'Brien, C. P. (1980). "Predicting the outcomes of psychotherapy: Findings of the Penn psychotherapy project." *Archives of General Psychiatry* 37(4): 471–481.

Luborsky, L., Singer, B., & Luborsky, L. (1975). "Comparative studies of psychotherapies." *Archives of General Psychiatry* 32: 995–1007.

Lynch, D. J. (1976). "A test of the complementarity hypothesis in AB research." *Journal of Consulting and Clinical Psychology* 44(5): 865. EJ146047.

Machell, D. F. (1987). "Fellowship as an important factor in alcoholism residential treatment." *Journal of Alcohol and Drug Education* 32(2): 56–58. EJ353577.

Macrae, J. F. (1980). "The influence of fee assessment on premature therapy termination." *Administration in Mental Health* 7(4): 282–291. EJ227443.

Magen, Z., & Aharoni, I. (1991). "Adolescents contributing towards others: Relationship to positive experiences and transpersonal commitment." *Journal of Humanistic Psychology* 31: 126–143.

Mallinckrodt, B. (1989). "Social support and the effectiveness of group therapy." *Journal of Counseling Psychology* 36(2): 170–175.

———. (1991). "Clients representations of childhood emotional bonds with parents, social support, and formation of the working alliance." *Journal of Counseling Psychology* 38(4): 401–409.

Maluccio, A. (1979). *Learning from Clients: Interpersonal Helping as Viewed by Clients and Social Workers.* New York: The Free Press.

Mann, B. J., & Borduin, C. M. (1991). "A critical review of psychotherapy outcome studies with adolescents." *Adolescence* 26(103): 505–541.

Manthei, R. J. (1980). *Development of a procedure for allowing mental health clients to choose their therapist.* Paper presented at the annual conference of the New Zealand Psychological Society, Dunedin. ED200848.

Markova, I., Forbes, C., & Inwood, M. (1984). "The consumers' views of genetic counseling in haemophilia." *American Journal of Medical Genetics* 17: 741–752.

Marks, A. M., Malizio, J., Hoch, J., Brody, R., & Fisher, M. (1983). "Assessment of health needs and willingness to utilise health care resources of adolescents in a suburban population." *Journal of Pediatrics* 102: 456–460.

Martin, G. A., McNair, D., & Hight, W. (1988). "Contributing factors to early premature termination at a college counseling center." *Journal of Counseling and Development* 66(5): 233–236. EJ368526.

Martin, J. (1987). "Cognitive mediation in person-centered rational–emotive therapy." *Journal of Counseling Psychology* 34(3): 251–260. EJ360530.

Martin, J., & Stelmaczonek, K. (1988). "Participants identification and recall of important events in counseling." *Journal of Counseling Psychology* 35(4): 385–390.

Marx, J. A., & Gelso, C. J. (1987). "Termination of individual counseling in a university counseling centre." *Journal of Counseling Psychology* 34(1): 3.

Masson, J. (1988). *Against Therapy*. London: Fontana/Collins.

Mather, S. R., & Rutherford, R. B. (1991). "Peer-mediated interventions promoting social skills of children and youth with behaviour disorders." *Education and Treatment of Children* 14(3): 227–242.

Matheson, G., Shue, K. L., & Bart, C. (1989). "A validation study of a short form hypnotic experience questionnaire and its relation to hypnotizability." *American Journal of Clinical Hypnosis* 32(1): 17–26.

Maurer, R. E., & Tindall, J. H. (1983). "Effects of postural congruence on client's perception of counselor empathy." *Journal of Counseling Psychology* 30(2): 158–163. EJ280778.

Mayer, J., & Timms, N. (1970). *The Client Speaks: Working Class Impressions of Casework*. London: Routledge & Keegan Paul.

McCarthy, P. R. (1982). "Differential effects of counselor self-referent responses and counselor status." *Journal of Counseling Psychology* 29: 125–131.

McGee, R., & Stanton, W. R. (1992). "Sources of distress among New Zealand adolescents." *Journal of Child Psychology and Psychiatry* 33(6): 999–1010.

McGee, R., Williams, S., Bradshaw, J., Chapel, J. L., Robins, A., & Silva, P. (1985). "The Rutter Scale for completion by teachers: Factor structure and relationships with cognitive abilities and family adversity in a sample of New Zealand children." *Journal of Child Psychology and Psychiatry* 26: 727–739.

McGuire, J. M., Parnell, T. F., Blau, B. I., & Abbott, D. W. (1994). "Demands for privacy amongst adolescents in multi-modal alchohol and drug-abuse treatments." *Journal of Counseling and Development* 73: 74–77.

McKinnon, D. G. (1990). "Client-preferred therapist sex-role orientations." *Journal of Counseling Psychology* 37(1): 10–15.

McLennan, J. (1988). "Conceptualising and measuring client-centered relationships." *Person-Centered Review* 3(3): 292–303.

———. (1991). "Formal and informal counselling help: Students' experiences." *British Journal of Guidance and Counselling* 19(2): 149–159.

McLeod, J. (1990). "The client's experience of counselling and psychotherapy: A review of the research literature." In D. Mearns & W. Dryden (Eds.), *Experiences of Counselling in Action*. London: Sage.

McNally, H. A. (1972). "An investigation of selected counselor and client characteristics as possible predictors." *Dissertation Abstracts International* A12: 6672–6673.

McNiell, B. W., May, R. J., & Lee, V. E. (1987). "Perceptions of counselor source characteristics by premature and successful terminators." *Journal of Counseling Psychology* 34(1): 86–89.

Mead, M. (1961). *Growing Up Young in Samoa*. New York: Morrow.

Meagher, J., & Clark, R. L. (1982). "Fewer adolescents discuss problems with school staff." *Phi Delta Kappan* (March): 494.

Mechanic, D. (Ed.). (1976). *The Growth of Bureaucratic Medicine*. New York: Wiley.

Medway, F. J. (1979). "Causal attributions for school-related problems: Teacher perceptions and teacher feedback." *Journal of Educational Psychology* 71: 809–818.

Meeus, W. (1989). "Parental and peer support in adolescence." In K. Hurrelman & U. Engel (Eds.), *The Social World of Adolescents*. Berlin: De Gruyter.

Mennicke, S. A., Lent, R. W., & Burgoyne, K. L. (1988). "Premature termination from university counseling centers: A review." *Journal of Counseling and Development* 66(10): 458–465. EJ379654.

Meyer, J. B. (1968). *Behavioural-reinforcement counseling with rural Wisconsin high-school youth*. Ph.D. dissertation, University of Wisconsin.

Meyer, J. B., Strowig, W., & Hasford, R. E. (1970). "Behavioural-reinforcement counseling with rural high-school youth." *Journal of Counseling Psychology* 17: 127.

Millen, L., & Roll, S. (1977). "Adolescent males ratings of being understood by fathers, best friends, and significant others." *Psychological Reports* 40: 1079–1082.

Miller, D., & Burt, R. A. (1982). "Children's rights on entering therapeutic institutions." *Child and Youth Services* 4: 89–98.

Mills, M. C. (1983). "Adolescents' self-disclosure in individual and group theme-centered modelling, reflecting, and probing interviews." *Psychological Reports* 53: 691–701.

———. (1985). "Adolescents' reactions to counseling interviews." *Adolescence* 20(77): 83–95.

———. (1987). "An intervention program for adolescents with behaviour problems." *Adolescence* 22(85): 91–96.

Mintz, J., Luborsky, L., & Auerbach, A. H. (1971). "Dimensions of psychotherapy: A factor-analytic study of ratings of psychotherapy sessions." *Journal of Consulting and Clinical Psychology* 36: 106–120.

Mooney, R. L. (1942). "Surveying high-school students' problems by means of a problem checklist." *Educational Research Bulletin* 21: 57–60.

Mooney, R. L., & Gordon, L. V. (1950). *Manual for the Mooney Problem Checklists*. New York: The Psychological Corporation.

Moos, R. H., & Trickett, E. J. (1974). *Classroom Environment Scale Manual*. Palo Alto, CA: Consulting Psychologists Press.

Morey, R. E., Miller, C. D., Fulton, R., Rosen, L. A., & Daly, J. L. (1989). "Peer counseling: Students served, problems discussed, overall satisfaction, and perceived helplessness." *The School Counselor* 37(2): 137–143.

Morita, H., Suzuki, M., Suzuki, I., & Kamoshita, S. (1993). "Psychiatric disorders in Japanese secondary school children." *Journal of Child Psychology and Psychiatry* 34(3): 317–332.

Morrison, L. A., & Shapiro, D. A. (1987). "Expectancy and outcome in prescriptive vs. exploratory therapy." *British Journal of Clinical Psychology* 26: 59–60.

Morten, G., & Atkinson, D. R. (1983). "Minority identity development and preference for counselor race." *Journal of Negro Education* 52: 156–162.

Murgatroyd, S. J. (1977). "Pupils perceptions of counselling: A case study." *British Journal of Guidance and Counselling* 5(1): 73–78.

Murray, C., & Thompson, F. (1985). "The representation of authority: An adolescent viewpoint." *Journal of Adolescence* 8: 217–229.

Musgrove, S. (1967). "University freshmen and their parents' attitudes." *Educational Research* 10(1): 78–80.

Mussen, P. H., Conger, J., & Kagan, J. (1970). *Child Development and Personality*. New York: Harper & Row.

Muus, R. E. (1975). *Theories of Adolescence* (3d ed.). New York: Random House.

Nadler, A. (1986a). "Self-esteem and the seeking and receiving of help: Theoretical and empirical perspectives. *Progress in Experimental Personality Research* 14: 115–163.

———. (1986b). "Help-seeking as a cultural phenomenon: Differences between city and Kibbutz dwellers." *Journal of Personality and Social Psychology* 51(5): 976–982.

———. (1987). "Determinants of help-seeking behaviour: The effects of helper's similarity, task centrality, and recipient's self-esteem." *European Journal of Social Psychology* 17: 57–67.

Nadler, A., & Porat, I. (1978). "When names do not help: Effects of anonymity and locus of need attribution on help-seeking behaviour." *Personality and Social Psychology Bulletin* 4: 624–626.

National Curriculum Council. (1988). *Circular Number One*. London: National Curriculum Council.

Neely, M. A., & Iburg, D. (1989). "Exploring high school counseling trends through critical incidents." *The School Counselor* 36(3): 179–185.

Nelson-Le Gall, S. A., & Gummerman, R. A. (1984). "Children's perceptions of helpers and helper motivation." *Journal of Applied Developmental Psychology* 5: 1–12.

Newfield, N. A., Joanning, H. P., Kuehl, B. P., & Quinn, W. H. (1991). "We can tell you about 'psychos' and 'shrinks': An ethnography of the family therapy of adolescent drug abuse" In T. C. Todd & M. D. Selekman (Eds.), *Family Therapy Approaches with Adolescent Substance Abusers*. Boston: Allyn & Bacon.

Newman, B. M. (1989). "The changing nature of the parent–adolescent relationship from early to late adolescence." *Adolescence* 24(96): 915–924.

Newman, I. M., Martin, G. L., & Petersen, C. (1978). *Attitudinal and normative factors associated with adolescent cigarette smoking*. Paper presented at the American Public Health Association, Los Angeles. ED166130.

Newport, J. M. (1977). "Guidance services in five secondary schools." *Delta* 20: 52–63.

Newton, F. B., & Caple, R. B. (1974). "Client and counselor preferences for counselor behaviour in the interview." *Journal of College Student Personnel* 15(3): 220–223. EJ097662.

Newton, J. (1988). *Preventing Mental Illness*. London: Routlege and Keegan Paul.

Noller, P., & Bagi, S. (1985). "Parent–adolescent communication." *Journal of Adolescence* 8: 125–144.

Noller, P., & Callan, V. J. (1990). "Adolescents' perceptions of the nature of their communications with parents." *Journal of Youth and Adolescence* 19(4): 349–361.

Northman, J. E. (1978). "Developmental changes in preferences for help." *Journal of Clinical Child Psychology* 7: 129–132

———. (1985). "The emergence of an appreciation for help during childhood and adolescence." *Adolescence* 20(80): 774–781.

Nurmi, J. E., Poole, M. E., & Kalakoski, V. (1994). "Age-differences in adolescent future-orientated goals, concerns, and related temporal extension in different cultural contexts." *Journal of Youth and Adolescence* 23(4): 471–487.

O'Brien, E., & Epstein, S. (1988). *The Multidimensional Self-Esteem Inventory: Professional Manual*. Odessa, FL: Psychological Assessment Resources.

Offer, D., Howard, K. I., Schonert, K. A., & Ostrov, J. D. (1991). "To whom do adolescents turn for help?" *Journal of the American Academy of Child and Adolescent Psychiatry* 30(4): 623–630.

Offer, D., & Offer, J. (1975). *From Teenage to Young Manhood: A Psychological Study*. New York: Basic Books.

Offer, D., Ostrov, E., & Howard, K. I. (1984). *Patterns of Adolescent Self-Image*. San Francisco: Jossey-Bass.

Offer, D., & Schonert-Reichl, A. (1992). "Debunking the myths of adolescence." *American Journal of Child and Adolescent Psychiatry* 31(6): 1003–1014.

Office for Standards in Education. (1992). *The Handbook for the Inspection of Schools*. London: Office of Her Majesty's Chief Inspector of Schools in England.

———. (1994). *16–19 guidance: A joint report by the Further Education Funding Council and the Office for Standards in Education*. London: Elizabeth House.

Offord, D. R., Boyle, M., Szatmari, P., Rae-Grant, N. I., Links, P. S., Cadman, D. T., Byles, J. A., Crawford, J. W., Blum, H. M., Byrne, C., Thomas, H., & Woodward, C. A. (1987). "Ontario child health study II: Six-month prevalence of disorder and rates of service utilisation." *Archives of General Psychiatry* 44: 832–837.

Oldfield, S. (1983). *The Counselling Relationship: A Study of the Client's Experience*. London: Routledge & Kegan Paul.

O'Leary, E. (1979). *The counselling relationship: Core conditions and core outcomes*. Unpublished Ph.D. dissertation, University College, Cork.

————. (1990). "Research on school counselling: An Irish perspective." *The School Counselor* 37(4): 261–269.

Olsen, J. E. (1975). *An analysis of short term training effects upon high school students' measured assertiveness.* Ph.D. dissertation, Purdue University.

Omizo, M. M., & Omizo, S. A. (1987). "The effects of eliminating self-defeating behaviour of learning-disabled children through group counseling." *The School Counselor* 34(4): 282–288.

————. (1988). "The effects of participation in group counseling sessions on self-esteem and locus of control among adolescents from divorced families." *The School Counselor* 36(1): 54–60.

————. (1989). "Art activities to improve self-esteem among native Hawaiian children." *Journal of Humanistic Education and Development* 27(4): 167–176. EJ398687.

Openheim, A. N. (1966). *Questionnaire Design and Attitude Measurement.* London: Heinemann.

Orlinski, D. E., & Howard, K. I. (1986). "The psychological interior of psychotherapy: Explorations with the Therapy Session Reports." In L. S. Greenberg & W. M. Pinsof (Eds.), *The Psychotherapeutic Process: A Research Process.* New York: Guilford.

Osborne, K. (1983). "Counselling requirements in a voluntary advice agency." *British Journal of Guidance and Counselling* 11(1): 82–85.

Ostrov, E. (1985). "The prevalence and characteristics of quietly disturbed adolescents in the community." In C. J. Brainerd & V. F. Reyna (Eds.), *Developmental Psychology.* The Hague: Elsevier Holland.

Otani, A. (1989a). "Client resistance to counseling: Its theoretical rationale and taxonomic classification." *Journal of Counseling and Development* 67(8): 458–461.

————. (1989b). "Resistance management techniques of Milton H. Erikson, M.D.: An application to non-hypnotic mental health counselling." *Journal of Mental Health Counseling* 11(4): 325–334.

Ottenbacher, K. J. (1991). "Statistical conclusion validity: An empirical analysis of multiplicity in mental retardation research." *American Journal of Mental Retardation* 95(4): 421–427.

Overbeck, A. L. (1977). "Life stress antecedents to application for help at a medical health center: A clinical study of adaptation." *Smith College Studies in Social Work* 47: 192–233.

Page, R. C., & Chandler, J. (1994). "Effects of group counseling on ninth grade at-risk students." *Journal of Mental Health Counseling* 16(3): 340–351.

Papini, D. R., Farmer, F. F., Clark, S. M., Micka, N., & Barnett, J. K. (1990). "Early adolescent age and gender differences in the pattern of emotional disclosure to parents and friends." *Adolescence* 15: 959–1001.

Paradise, L. V. (1978). *The relationship between client reluctance and counseling effectiveness.* Paper presented at the annual meeting of the American Educational Research Association, Toronto. ED156976.

Paradise, L. V., & Wilder, D. H. (1979). "The relationship between client reluctance and counseling effectiveness." *Counselor Education and Supervision* 19(1): 35–40. EJ209163.

Parker, H. C. (1974). "Contingency management and concomitant changes in elementary students' self-concepts." *Psychology in the Schools* 11(1): 70–79.

Parker-Jenkins, M. (1995). "Pupil empowerment: Pupil power?" *Pastoral Care* (June).

Parkum, K. H. (1985). "The impact of chaplaincy services in selected hospitals in the eastern United States." *Journal of Pastoral Care* 39(3): 262–269.

Paterson, J. E., Field, J., & Pryor, J. (1994). "Adolescent perceptions of their attachment relationships with their mothers, fathers, and friends." *Journal of Youth and Adolescence* 23(5): 579–599.

Patten, M. I., & Walker, L. G. (1990). "Marriage guidance counselling: 1. What clients think." *British Journal of Guidance and Counselling* 18(1): 29–39.

Patterson, J. M., & McGubbin, H. I. (1987). "Adolescent coping style and behaviours: Conceptualisation and measurement." *Journal of Adolescence* 10: 163–186.

Payne, B. D., & Manning, B. H. (1991). "Self-talk of student teachers and resulting relationships." *Journal of Educational Research* 85(10): 47–51.

Peel, J. L., & Dansereau, D. F. (1998). "Management and prevention of personal problems in older adolescents via schematic maps and peer feedback." *Adolescence* 33(130): 355–374.

Perlman, R. (1975). *Consumers and Social Services.* New York: John Wiley.

Persson, G. (1976). "Non-pharmacological factors in drug treatment of anxiety states." *Acta Psychiatrica Scandinavia* 54: 238–247.

Persson, G., & Nordlund, C. L. (1983). "Expectations of improvement and attitudes to treatment processes in relation to outcome with four treatment methods for phobic disorders. *Acta Psychiatrica Scandinavia* 68: 484–493.

Petersen, A. C. (1988). "Adolescent development." *Annual Review of Psychology* 39: 583–607.

Phares, V., & Compas, B. E. (1992). "The role of fathers in child and adolescent psychopathology: Make room for daddy." *Psychological Bulletin* 111(3): 387–412.

Phelps, S. B., & Jarvis, P. A. (1994). "Coping in adolescence: Empirical evidence for a theoretically based approach to assessing coping." *Journal of Youth and Adolescence* 23(3): 359–371.

Pitman, J. F., & Bowen, G. L. (1994). "Adolescents on the move." *Youth and Society* 26(1): 69–91.

Ponterotto, J. G. (1987). "Counseling Mexican Americans: A multi-modal approach." *Journal of Counseling and Development* 65: 308–312.

———. (1988). "An organisational framework for understanding the role of culture in counseling." *Journal of Counseling and Development* 66: 237–241.

Ponterotto, J. G., Alexander, C. M., & Hinkston, J. A. (1988). "Afro-American preferences for counselor characteristics: A replication and extension." *Journal of Counseling Psychology* 35(2): 172–182.

Ponterotto, J. G., & Benesch, K. F. (1988). "An organisational framework for understanding the role of culture in counseling." *Journal of Counseling and Development* 66: 237–241.

Ponterotto, J. G., & Furlong, M. J. (1985). "Evaluating counselor effectiveness: A critical review of rating scale instruments." *Journal of Counseling Psychology* 32(4): 597–616.

Pope, A. W., McHale, S. M., & Craighead, W. E. (1988). *Self-Esteem Enhancement with Children and Adolescents.* New York: Pergamon.

Poppen, B., & Peters, H. (1965). "Expectations of junior high school pupils about counseling." *Journal of Educational Research* 58: 358–361.

Porche, L. M., & Banikiotes, P. G. (1982). "Racial and attitudinal factors affecting the perceptions of counselors by black students." *Journal of Counseling Psychology* 29: 169–174.

Porteous, M. A. (1985). "Developmental aspects of adolescent problem disclosure in England and Ireland." *Journal of Child Psychology and Psychiatry* 26(3): 465–478.

Porteous, M. A., & Fisher, C. J. (1980). "Counseling, support and advice: The adolescent viewpoint." *British Journal of Guidance and Counselling* 8(1): 67–75.

Porteous, M. A., & Kelleher, E. (1987). "School climate differences and problem admission in secondary schools." *British Journal of Guidance and Counselling* 15(1): 72–81.

Potamianos, G., Gorman, D. M., Duffy, S. W., & Peters, T. (1984). "The use of the Severity of Alcohol Dependency Questionnaire (SADQ) on a sample of problem drinkers presenting to a district general hospital." *Alcohol* 1(6): 441–445.

Prajer, E., & Blum, A. (1980). "A client-developed self-assessment measure." *Rehabilitation Counseling Bulletin* 23(3): 227–229. EJ221229.

Price, L. Z., & Iverson, M. A. (1969). "Students perceptions of counselors with varying statuses and role behaviours in the initial interview." *Journal of Counseling Psychology* 16(6): 469–474.

Prospero, M. K. (1987). *Effects of confirmation versus disconfirmation of counselor directiveness in students with congruent expectations and preferences.* Unpublished Ph.D. dissertation, University of Akron.

Quarmby, M. (1993). "Peer counseling with bereaved adolescents." *British Journal of Guidance and Counselling* 21(2): 196–211.

Quarter, J. J., & Laxer, R. M. (1970). "A structured program of teaching and counseling for conduct problem students in a junior high school." *Journal of Educational Research* 63: 229–231.

Quintana, S. M., & Meara, N. M. (1990). "Internalisation of therapeutic relationships in short-term counseling." *Journal of Counseling Psychology* 37(2): 123–130.

Raffaelli, M., & Duckett, E. (1989). "We were just talking . . .: Conversations in early adolescence." *Journal of Youth and Adolescence* 18(6): 567–581.

Raja, S. N., McGee, R., & Stanton, W. R. (1991). "Perceived attachments to parents and peers and psychological well-being in adolescence." *Journal of Youth and Adolescence* 21: 471–485.

Raviv, A., Bar-Tal, D., Raviv, A., & Peleg, D. (1990). "Perception of epistemic authorities by children and adolescents." *Journal of Youth and Adolescence* 19: 495–510.

Raviv, A., Raviv, R., & Arnon, G. (1991). "Psychological counselling over the radio: Listening motivations and the threat to self-esteem." *Journal of Applied Social Psychology* 21(4): 253–269.

Raviv, A., Raviv, R., & Yunovitz, R. (1989). "Radio psychology and psychotherapy: Comparison of client attitudes and expectations." *Professional Psychology: Research and Practice* 20(2): 67–72.

Reagles, K. W. (1970). "Correlates of client satisfaction in an expanded vocational rehabilitation programme." Wisconsin Studies in Vocational Rehabilitation; Monograph X11, Series 2. Regional Rehabilitation Research Institute, University of Wisconsin. ED046008.

———. (1972a). "Development of a scale of client satisfaction for clients receiving vocational rehabilitation counseling services." *Rehabilitation Research and Practice Review* 3(2): 15–22. EJ062605.

———. (1972b). "Client satisfaction as a function of interventive counselor behaviours." *Rehabilitation Research and Practice Review* 3(2): 23–29. EJ061538.

Reber, A. S. (1985). *The Penguin Dictionary of Psychology*. London: Penguin.

Rednar, R. l., & Parker, C. A. (1969). *Client susceptibility to persuasion and counseling outcome*. Paper presented at the American Psychological Association convention, Washington, DC.

Reid, I. (1977). "Sunday school attendance and moral attitudes, knowledge and practice." *Learning for Living* 17: 3–8.

———. (1980). *Sunday Schools: A Suitable Case for Treatment*. London: Chester House.

Reid, K. (1989). "Helping troubled pupils: Grassroots realities." In K. Reid (Ed.), *Helping Troubled Pupils in Secondary Schools* (Volume 1). Oxford: Blackwell.

Reisman, J. M., & Shorr, S. I. (1978). "Friendship claims and expectations among children and adults." *Child Development* 49: 913–916.

Remley, T. P., & Albright, P. L. (1988). "Expectations for middle school counselors: Views of students, teachers, principals, and parents." *The School Counselor* 35(4): 290–296.

Rennie, D. (1985a). *An early return from interviews with clients about their therapy interviews: The functions of the narrative*. Paper presented at the thirty-fourth annual meeting of the Ontario Psychological Association, Ottawa.

Rhode, P., & Bellfield, K. (1992). *The Next Generation*. Minneapolis: Urban Coalition of Minneapolis.

Rice, L., & Greenberg, L. (Eds.). (1984). *Patterns of Change: Intensive Analysis of the Psychotherapy Process*. New York: Guilford.

Richardson, B. K. (1973). "Client–counselor interactions/patterns of service–client outcome: Rehabilitation counselor interview behaviour and client outcome in a comprehensive rehabilitation facility." Arkansas Studies in Vocation Rehabilitation; Series 1. Arkansas Rehabilitation Research and Training Center, Arkansas University. ED123546.

Richman, C. L., Clark, M. L., & Brown, K. P. (1985). "General and specific self-esteem in late adolescent students: Race x gender x SES effects." *Adolescence* 20(79): 555–566.

Rickabaugh, K. W. (1972). "Counselor comfort, counseling, climate, and client satisfaction: Client ratings and academic improvement." *Counselor Education and Supervision* 11(3): 219–223. EJ051517.

Rickwood, D. J. (1992). *Help seeking of psychological problems in late adolescence*. Unpublished Ph.D. dissertation, Australian National University, Canberra, Australia.

Ridgway, I. R., & Sharpley, C. F. (1990). "Empathic interactional sequences and counselor trainee effectiveness." *Counselling Psychology Quarterly* 3(3): 257–265.

Riordan, R. J. (1978). "Helping counselors minimise client reluctance." *Counselor Education and Supervision* 18(1): 6–13. EJ189992.

Rivenbark, W. H. (1971). "Self-disclosure patterns amongst adolescents." *Psychological Reports* 28: 35–42.

Robiner, W. N., & Storandt, M. (1983). "Client perceptions of the therapeutic relationship as a function of client and counselor age." *Journal of Counseling Psychology* 30: 96–99.

Robinson, S. E., Morrow, S., Kigin, T., & Lindeman, M. (1991). "Peer counselors in a high school setting: Evaluation of training and impact on students." *The School Counselor* 39(1): 35–40.

Robinson, W. P. (1990). "Academic achievement and self-esteem in secondary schools: Muddles, myths, and reality." *Educational Research and Perspectives* 17(1): 3–21.

Robson, C. (1993). *Real World Research: A Resource for Social Scientists and Practitioner Researchers*. Oxford: Blackwell.

Roffey, S., Majors, K., & Tarrant, T. (1997). "Friends—who needs them? What do we know and what can we do?" *Educational and Child Psychology* 14(3): 51–56.

Rogers, C. R. (1957). "The necessary and sufficient conditions of therapeutic personality change." *Journal of Consulting Psychology* 21: 95–103.

Rose, A. (1978). "The effects of self-instruction on the self-concept of children with learning problems." *Dissertation Abstracts International* A39(5): 2761.

Rosen, A., & Rujla, O. (1984). "Client locus of control, problem perception, and interview behaviour." *Journal of Counseling Psychology* 31(3): 314–321.

Rosenberg, M. (1965). *Society and Adolescent Self-Image*. Princeton, NJ: Princeton University Press.

———. (1976). "Which significant others?" In J. Hess (Ed.), *Family Roles and Interaction: An Anthology* (2d ed.). Chicago: Rand McNally.

———. (1985). "Self concept and psychological well-being in adolescence." In T. Leahy (Ed.), *The Development of the Self*. New York: Academic Press.

———. (1986). "Self-concept from middle childhood through adolescence." In J. Suls & A. G. Greenwald (Eds.), *Psychological Perspectives on the Self* (Volume 3). Hillsdale, NJ: Erlbaum.

Rubin, S. E. (1973). "Client–counselor interactions/patterns of service-client outcome: A report on rehabilitation facility client outcome." Arkansas Studies in Vocation Rehabilitation; Series 1. Arkansas Rehabilitation Research and Training Center, University of Arkansas. ED123545.

Rutter, M. (1977). *Helping Troubled Children*. Rickmansworth, U.K.: Penguin.

Rutter, M., Cox, A., Tupling, C., Berger, M., & Yule, W. (1975). "Attainment in two geographical areas: 1. The prevalence of psychiatric disorder." *British Journal of Psychiatry* 126: 520–533.

Ryan, M., Stiller, J. D., & Lynch, J. H. (1994). "Representations of relationships to teachers, parents, and friends as predictors of academic motivation and self-esteem." *Journal of Adolescence* 14(2): 226–249.

Ryan, V. L., & Gizynski, M. N. (1971). "Behaviour therapy in retrospect: Patients' feelings about their behaviour therapy." *Journal of Consulting and Clinical Psychology* 37(1): 1–9.

Sakahura, S., Sano, H., & Fukushima, O. (1993). "The effects of counseling training: Study on the differences among teachers with training, regular teachers, and guidance teachers." *Japanese Journal of Counseling Science* 26(2): 139–145.

Saleh, M. A. (1987). "Guidance and counselling in the kingdom of Saudi Arabia." *International Journal for the Advancement of Counselling* 10: 277–286.

Sanchez, A. R., & Atkinson, D. R. (1983). "Mexican–American cultural commitment, preference for counselor ethnicity, and willingness to use counseling." *Journal of Counseling Psychology* 30: 215–220.

Sanchez, M. (1969). *The effects of client-centered group counseling on self concept and certain attitudes of seventh and eighth grade students*. Ph.D. dissertation, United States International University.

Sanders, A., & Sanders, J. (1985). "Faculty members and students perceptions of services provided by their counseling center." *College Student Journal* 19(4): 384–388.

Santoro, D. A. (1970). *Perceptions of interview behaviour and relationships in counseling supervision*. Paper presented at the American Research Association convention, Washington, DC. ED039548.

Sarason, I. G., & Ganzer, V. J. (1973). "Modelling and group discussion in the rehabilitation of juvenile delinquents." *Journal of Counseling Psychology* 20: 442–449.

Schover, L. R. (1980). *Gender differences in therapist responses to client sexual material*. Paper presented at the eighty-eighth annual convention of the American Psychological Association, Montreal. ED201915.

Schreisheim, C. A., & Hill, K. D. (1981). "Controlling acquiescence response bias by item reversals: The effect on response validity." *Educational and Psychological Measurement* 41(4): 1101–1114.

Schwartz, A. J., & Bernard, H. S. (1981). "Comparison of patient and therapist evaluation of time-limited psychotherapy." *Psychotherapy Theory, Research and Practice* 18(1): 101–108.

Sciarra, D. T., & Ponterotto, J. G. (1991). "Counselling the Hispanic bilingual family: Challenges to the therapeutic process." *Psychotherapy* 28: 473–479.

Scogin, F. (1986). "Mental health services in a rural clinic: A retrospective study of length of stay and premature termination in psychotherapy." *Journal of Rural Community Psychology* 7(1): 35–44. EJ347919.

Sebald, H. (1986). "Adolescents' shifting orientation towards parents and peers: A curvilinear trend over recent decades." *Journal of Marriage and the Family* 48: 5–13.

———. (1989). "Adolescents' peer orientation: Changes in the support system during the past three decades." *Adolescence* 24(96): 937–946.

Sebald, H., & White, B. (1980). "Teenagers divided reference groups: Uneven alignment with parents and peers." *Adolescence* 15(60): 979–984.

Segovia, J., Bartlett, R. F., & Edwards, A. C. (1989). "An empirical analysis of the 'Dimensions of Health Status' measures." *Social Science and Medicine* 29(6): 761–768.

Seifert, K. H. (1985). "Evaluation of guidance and counseling in Austria." *International Journal for the Advancement of Counseling* 8: 55–73.

Seiffge-Krenke, I. (1990). "Developmental processes in self-concept and coping behaviour." In H. Bosma & S. Jackson (Eds.), *Coping and Self-Concept in Adolescence.* Berlin: Springer.

Shafer, R. (1967). *Projective Testing and Psychoanalysis.* New York: International Universities Press.

Shaffer, P., Murillo, N., & Micheal, W. B. (1981). "A comparison of factor dimensions in revised scales for student client evaluation of counselors in a university counseling and testing center." *Educational and Psychological Measurement* 41(2): 473–477.

Shapiro, D. A. (1976). "The effects of therapeutic conditions: Positive results re-visited." *British Journal of Medical Psychology* 49(4): 315–323.

Shapiro, E. G. (1980). "Is seeking help from a friend like seeking help from a stranger?" *Social Psychology Quarterly* 43: 259–263.

Sharkin, B. S. (1988). "The measurement and treatment of client anger in counselling." *Journal of Counseling and Development* 66(8): 361–365. EJ398700.

———. (1989). "How counselor trainees respond to client anger: A review." *Journal of Counseling and Development* 67(10): 561–564. EJ398700.

Shell, R. M., & Eisenberg, N. (1992). "A developmental model of recipients' reactions to aid." *Psychological Bulletin* 111(3): 413–433.

Shore, M., & Massimo, J. (1966). "Comprehensive, vocationally-oriented psychotherapy for adolescent boys: A follow-up study." *American Journal of Orthopsychiatry* 36: 609–615.

Shueman, S. A. (1980). "Client satisfaction with intake: Is the waiting list all that matters?" *Journal of College Student Personnel* 21(2): 114–121. EJ220959.

Siann, G., Draper, J., & Cosford, B. (1982). "Pupils as consumers: Perceptions of guidance and counselling in a Scottish school." *British Journal of Guidance and Counselling* 10(1): 51–61.

Siefge-Krenke, I. (1990). "Developmental processes in self-concept and coping behaviour." In H. Bosma & S. Jackson (Eds.), *Coping and Self-Concept in Adolescence.* Berlin: Springer.

Silove, D., Parker, G., & Manicavasagar, V. (1990). "Perceptions of general and specific therapist behaviours." *Journal of Nervous and Mental Disease* 178(5): 292–299.

Silverman, M. S. (1969). "Effects of differential practicum experiences on client and counselor perceptions of initial interviews." ED044720.

———. (1973). "Practicum perceptions of initial interviews: Client–counselor divergence." *Counselor Education and Supervision* 13(2): 158–161. EJ089256.

Silverman, W. H., & Beech, R. P. (1984). "Length of intervention and assumed client outcome." *Journal of Clinical Psychology* 40(2): 475–480.

Simoni, J. M., Adelman, H. S., & Perry, N. (1991). "Perceived control, causality, expectations, and help-seeking behaviour." *Counseling Psychology Quarterly* 4(1): 37–44.

Simons, J. A., & Helms, J. E. (1976). "Influence of counselors' marital status, sex, and age on college and non-college womens' counselor preference." *Journal of Counseling Psychology* 23: 380–386.

Simpson, R. L. (1962). "Parental influence, anticipatory socialisation and social mobility." *American Sociological Review* 27: 517–522.

Sinha, V. (1972). "Age-differences in self-disclosure." *Developmental Psychology* 7: 257–258.

Sinnett, E. R., & Danskin, D. H. (1967). "Intake and walk-in procedure in a college counseling setting." *Personnel and Guidance Journal* 45: 445–451.

Sishta, S. K., Rinco, S., & Sullivan, J.C.F. (1986). "Clients' satisfaction survey in a psychiatric inpatient population attached to a general hospital." *Canadian Journal of Psychiatry* 31(2): 123–128.

Skuy, M., Hoar, R., Oakley-Smith, T., & Westaway, M. (1985). "Perceptions of the guidance teacher as preferred helping agent in some South African schools." *British Journal of Guidance and Counselling* 13(3): 266–274.

Smith, M., Glass, G., & Miller, T. (1980). *The Benefits of Psychotherapy.* Baltimore: Johns Hopkins University Press.

Smith, P. K. (1991). "The silent nightmare: Bullying and victimisation in school peer groups." *The Psychologist* 4: 243–248.

Smith, T. E. (1976). "Push versus pull: Intra-family versus peer-group variables as possible determinants of adolescent orientation to parents." *Youth Society* 8: 5–26.

Snoek, D., & Rothblum, E. (1979). "Self-disclosure amongst adolescents in relation to parent affection and control patterns." *Adolescence* 14(54): 333–340.

Soares, A. T., & Soares, L. M. (1974). *Significant others and self-perception of disadvantaged students.* Paper presented at the annual meeting of the American Educational Research Association, Chicago. ED094025.

Solantaus, T., Rimpela, M., & Rakhonen, O. (1985). "Social epidemiology of the experience of threat of war among Finnish youth." *Social Science and Medicine* 21: 145–151.

Southern Regional Education Board. (1979). *Client outcome evaluation in mental health centers.* Rockville, MD: Division of Manpower and Training Programs, National Institute of Mental Health. ED185482.

Spirito, A., Stark, L. J., Grace, N., & Stamoulis, D. (1991). "Common problems and coping strategies reported in childhood and early adolescence." *Journal of Youth and Adolescence* 20(5): 531–544.

Sproles, E. K. (1988). "Research indicates new approaches for counseling vocational education students." *The School Counselor* 36(1): 8–23.

SPSS. (1994). *SPSS for Windows 6.1.* Chertsey, Surrey: SPSS.

Stacey, F., Eggeman, K., Eggeman, B. S., Moxley, V., & Schumm, W. R. (1986). "Premarital counseling as perceived by newlywed couples: An exploratory study." *Journal of Sex and Marital Therapy* 12(3): 221–228.

Stamler, V. L., Christiansen, M. D., Staley, K. H., & Macagno-Shang, L. (1991). "Client preferences for counselor gender." *Psychology of Women Quarterly* 15(2): 317–321.

Stark, L. J., Spirito, A., Williams, C., & Guevremont, D. (1989). "Common problems and coping strategies. 1: Findings with normal adolescents." *Journal of Abnormal and Child Psychology* 17: 203–212.

Steenbarger, B. N. (1992). "Toward science-practice integration in brief counseling and psychotherapy." *The Counseling Psychologist* 20(3): 403–450.

Steinberg, L., & Silverberg, S. B. (1986). "The vicissitudes of autonomy in early adolescence." *Child Development* 57: 841–851.

Stern, S. L. (1975). "Confounding of personality and social class characteristics in research on premature termination." *Journal of Consulting and Clinical Psychology* 43(3): 341–344. EJ120574.

Stewart, R. M. (1986). "Written versus videotaped pre-counseling training of clients." *Counselor Education and Supervision* 25(3): 197–209. EJ334035.

Stiles, W. B. (1980). "Measurement of the impact of psychotherapy sessions." *Journal of Consulting and Clinical Psychology* 48: 176–185.

Stiles, W. B., Shapiro, D. A., & Elliott, R. (1986). "Are all psychotherapies equivalent?" *American Psychologist* 41: 1165–1180.

Stiles, W. B., Shapiro, D. A., & Firth-Cozens, J. A. (1988). "Do sessions of different treatments have different impacts?" *Journal of Counseling Psychology* 35(4): 391–396.

Stiles, W. B., & Snow, J. S. (1984). "Counseling session impact as viewed by novice counselors and their clients." *Journal of Counseling Psychology* 31(1): 3–12.

Stockton, R. (1981). "Identifying the group drop-out: A review of the literature." *Journal for Specialists in Group Work* 6(2): 75–82. EJ248196.

Strong, S. R., Hendel, D. D., & Bratton, J. C. (1971). "College students' views of campus help-givers: Counselors, advisers, and psychiatrists." *Journal of Counseling Psychology* 18(2): 234–238.

Strupp, H., Wallach, M., & Wogan, M. (1964). "Psychotherapy experience in retrospect: Questionnaire surveys of former patients and their therapists." *Psychological Monographs: General & Applied* 78 (11, Whole No. 588).

Strupp, H., Fox, R., & Lessler, K. (1969). *Patients View Their Psychotherapy.* Baltimore: Johns Hopkins University Press.

Stuart-Smith, C. (1994). "Reactions to Hill-End Adolescent Unit; Interviews with twenty ex-patients." *Adolescence* 17: 483–489.

Subich, L. M., & Coursol, D. H. (1985). "Counseling expectations of clients and non-clients for group and individual treatment modes." *Journal of Counseling Psychology* 32: 245–251.

Suzuki, R. (1989). "Adolescents' dropout from individual psychotherapy—is it true?" *Journal of Adolescence* 12: 197–205.

Switzer, G. E., Simmons, R. G., Dew, M. A., Regalski, J. M., & Wang, C. H. (1995). "The effect of a school-based helper programme on adolescent self-image, attitudes, and behaviour." *Journal of Early Adolescence* 15(4): 429–455.

Szagun, G. (1992). "Children's Understanding of the feeling experience and causes of sympathy." *Journal of Child Psychology and Psychiatry* 33(7): 1183–1191.

Tabberer, R. (1984). "Introducing study skills at 16–19." *Educational Research* 26(1): 1–6.

Taveggia, T. (1974). "Resolving research controversy through empirical cumulation." *Sociological Methods and Research* 2: 395–407.

Taylor, L., Adelman, H. S., & Kayser-Boyd, N. (1985). "Exploring minors' reluctance and dissatisfaction with psychotherapy." *Professional Psychology: Research and Practice* 16(3): 418–425.

———. (1986). "The origin climate questionnaire as a tool for studying therapeutic process." *Journal of Child and Adolescent Psychotherapy* 3(1): 10–16.

Terrell, F., & Terrell, S. (1984). "Race of counselor, client sex, cultural mistrust level, and premature termination from counseling among black clients." *Journal of Counseling Psychology* 31(3): 371–375. EJ305201.

Tessler, R. C. (1975). "Clients' reactions to initial interviews: Determinants of relationship centered and problem-centered satisfaction." *Journal of Counseling Psychology* 22: 187–191.

Thrower, J. H., & Tyler, J. D. (1986). "Edwards Personal Preferences Schedule correlates of addiction counselor effectiveness." *International Journal of the Addictions* 21: 2.

Timms, N., & Blampied, A. (1985). *Intervention in Marriage: The Experience of Counselors and Their Clients*. Joint Unit For Social Services Research, University of Sheffield.

Tinsley, D. J., Hinson, J. A., Holt, M. S., & Tinsley, H.E.A. (1990). "Level of psychosocial development, perceived level of psychological difficulty, counseling readiness, and expectations about counseling: Examination of group differences." *Journal of Counseling Psychology* 37(2): 143–148.

Tinsley, D. J., Holt, M. S., Hinson, J. A., & Tinsley, H.E.A. (1991). "A construct validation study of the Expectations About Counseling—Brief Form: Factorial validity." *Measurement and Evaluation in Counseling and Development* 24: 101–110.

Tinsley, H.E.A. (1982). "Expectations about counseling." Unpublished manuscript, Department of Psychology, University of Southern Illinois.

———. (1992). "Am I the fifth horseman of the apocalypse?: Comments on research concerning expectations about counseling." *Journal of Counseling Psychology* 39(1): 59–65.

Tinsley, H.E.A., & Benton, B. L. (1978). "Expectations in counseling." *Journal of College Student Personnel* 19: 537–543.

Tinsley, H.E.A., Bowman, S. L., & Ray, S. B. (1988). "Manipulation of expectancies about counseling and psychotherapy: Review and analysis of expectancy manipulation strategies and results." *Journal of Counseling Psychology* 35(1): 99–108.

Tinsley, H.E.A., De St. Aubin, T., & Brown, M. T. (1982). "College students' help-seeking preferences." *Journal of Counseling Psychology* 29(5): 523–533.

Tinsley, H.E.A., & Westcot, A. M. (1990). "Analysis of the cognitions stimulated by the items on the Expectations About Counseling—Brief Form: An analysis of construct validity." *Journal of Counseling Psychology* 37(2): 223–226.

Tojyo, M., & Maeda, M. (1993). "The effects of counseling training for teachers." *Japanese Journal of Counseling Science* 26(1): 45–53.

Tourville, J. N., & Bowen, G. L. (1994). "The quality of the parent–child relationship and adolescents' willingness to turn to same-sex peers for help in times of trouble." *Journal of Social Behaviour and Personality* (9): 259–269.

Tracey, T. J. (1986). "Interactional correlates of premature termination." *Journal of Consulting and Clinical Psychology* 54(6): 784–788. EJ348845.

Trepper, T. (1991). Editorial comment in N. Worden, *Adolescents and Their Families: An introduction to Assessment and Intervention*. New York: Hayworth Press.

Truax, C. B. (1971a). "Degree of negative transference occurring in group psychotherapy and client outcome in juvenile delinquents." *Journal of Clinical Psychology* 27(1): 132–136. EJ031180.

————. (1971b). "Counselor focus on client anxiety source and client outcome in juvenile delinquents." *Canadian Counselor* 5(3): 57–60. EJ032950.

Truax, C. B., & Carkhuff, R. R. (1967). *Towards Effective Counseling and Psychotherapy*. Chicago: Aldine.

Tryon, G. S. (1984). "Problems commuters, residence hall students, and students from different years bring to counseling." *College Student Journal* 18(3): 215–221.

————. (1988). *Relationship of therapist attitudes at intake to client premature termination*. Paper presented at the annual meeting of the Eastern Psychological Association, Buffalo. ED300691.

————. (1990). "Session depth and smoothness in relation to the concept of engagement in counseling." *Journal of Counseling Psychology* 37(3): 248–253.

Tryon, G. S., & Kane, A. S. (1990). "The helping alliance and premature termination." *Counseling Psychology Quarterly* 3(3): 233–238.

Tucker, C. M. (1980). *Client-centered problem-solving networks in complex organisations*. Paper presented at the annual meeting of the Central States Speech Association, Chicago. ED193699.

Tuma, J. (1989). "Mental health services for children: The state of the art." *American Psychologist* 44: 188–199.

Turner, R. G., & Keyson, M. (1978). "Relationships between client self-perceptions of self-conscious levels and therapist awareness of these perceptions." *Journal of Consulting and Clinical Psychology* 46(6): 1586–1587. EJ221150.

Tyler, F. B., & Gatz, M. (1977). "Development of individual psychosocial competence in a high school setting." *Journal of Consulting and Clinical Psychology* 45: 441–449.

Tyler, L. E. (1964). "The antecedents of two varieties of vocational interests." *Genetic Psychology Monographs* 70: 177–227.

Vandecreek, L., & Angstadt, L. (1985). "Client preferences and anticipations about counselor self-disclosure." *Journal of Counseling Psychology* 32(2): 206–214.

Vandewiele, M. (1979). "Problems of secondary school students in Senegal." *Journal of Psychology* 103: 113–120.

Van Hoose, W. H. (1969). "The efficacy of counselling in the elementary school." ED033394.

Van Riper, B. W. (1971). "Student perception: The counsellor is what he does." *The School Counselor* 19: 53–56.

Verhulst, F. C., & Van der Ende, J. (1992). "Agreement between parents' reports and adolescent self-reports of problem behaviour." *Journal of Child Psychology and Psychiatry* 33(6): 1011–1023.

Vial-Val, G., Rosenthal, R. H., Curtiss, G., & Marohn, R. C. (1984). "Dropout from adolescent psychotherapy: A preliminary study." *Journal of the American Academy of Child Psychiatry* 23: 562–568.

Vikan, A. (1985). "Psychiatric epidemiology in a sample of 1,510 ten year old children." *Journal of Child Psychology and Psychiatry* 26: 55–75.

Viney, L. L., Clarke, A. M., Bunn, T. A., & Benjamin, Y. N. (1986). "Crisis-intervention counseling: An evaluation of long and short-term effects." *Journal of Counseling Psychology* 32(1): 29–39.

Violato, C., & Holden, W. B. (1988). "A confirmatory factor analysis of a four-factor model of adolescent concerns." *Journal of Youth and Adolescence* 17(10): 101–112.

Volsky, T., Magoon, T., Norman, W., & Hoyt, D. (1965). *The Outcomes of Psychotherapy: Theory and Research.* Minneapolis: University of Minnesota Press.

Wachowiak, D., & Diaz, S. (1982). *Interpersonal attraction in the counseling relationship.* Paper presented at the twenty-eighth annual meeting of the South-eastern Psychological Association, New Orleans. ED219660.

Wachtel, P. L. (1982). *Resistance: Psychodynamic and Behavioral Approaches.* New York: Plenum.

Wade, B., & Moore, M. (1993). *Experiencing Special Education.* Budkingham: Open University Press.

Wagner, W. G. (1994). "Counseling with childen: An opportunity for tomorrow." *The Counseling Psychologist* 22(3): 381–401.

Waitzkin, H. (1984). "Doctor–patient communication: Clinical implications of social scientific research." *Journal of the American Medical Association* 252(17): 2441–2446.

———. (1985). "Information giving in medical care." *Journal of Health and Social Behaviour* 26: 81–101.

————. (1989). "A critical theory of medical discourse: Ideology, social control, and the processing of social context in medical encounters." *Journal of Health and Social Behaviour* 30: 220–239.

Wakefield, J. F. (1996). *Educational Psychology: Learning to Be a Problem Solver*. Boston: Houghton Mifflin.

Walker, J. A., Harris, L., Blum, R., Schneider, B. J., & Resnick, M. (1990). *Outlooks and Insights: Understanding Rural Adolescents*. Minneapolis: University of Minnesota Press.

Walster, E., & Walster, G. W. (1978). *Equity: Theory and Research*. Boston: Allyn & Bacon.

Walters, R. P. (1985). "A survey of client satisfaction in a lay counseling program." *Journal of Psychology and Christianity* 6(2): 62–69.

Wang, W. (1987). "The effect of a peer counsellor's training programme in a senior high school." *Bulletin of Educational Psychology* 20: 205–227.

Warchal, P., & Southern, S. (1986). "Perceived importance of counselling among adult students." *Journal of College Student Personnel* 27(1): 43–48.

Watkins, C. E., Savickas, M. L., Brizzi, J., & Manus, M. (1990). "Effects of counselor response behaviour on clients' impressions during vocational counseling." *Journal of Counseling Psychology* 37(2): 138–142.

Weibe, B., & Williams, J. D. (1972). "Self-disclosure to parents by high-school seniors." *Psychological Reports* 31: 690.

Weisberg, H. F., & Bowen, B. D. (1977). *An Introduction to Survey Research and Data Analysis*. London: Sage.

Weisz, J. R., Weiss, B., & Donenberg, G. R. (1992). "The lab versus the clinic: Effects of child and adolescent psychotherapy." *American Psychologist* (December): 1578–1585.

Wells, C. E., & Ritter, K. Y. (1979). "Paperwork, pressure, and discouragement: Student attitudes towards guidance services and implications for the profession." *Personnel and Guidance Journal* 58: 170–175.

Wells, P. G., Morris, A., Jones, R. M., & Allen, D. J. (1978). "An adolescent unit assessed: A consumer survey." *British Journal of Psychiatry* 132: 300–308.

West, J. S., Kayser, L., Overton, P., & Saltmarsh, R. (1991). "Student perceptions that inhibit the initiation of counseling." *The School Counselor* 39(2): 77–83.

West, L. (1975). "Some implications of self-disclosure studies for group counselling with adolescents." *Canadian Counselor* 4: 57–62.

West, L. W., & Zingle, H. W. (1969). "A self-disclosure inventory for adolescents." *Psychological Reports* 24: 439–445.

Westwood, M. J. (1982). "A cross-cultural comparison of East Indian and Anglo-European expectations of counseling." *International Journal for the Advancement of Counselling* 5: 283–289.

Whitaker, A., Lohnson, J., Shaffer, D., Rappoport, J. L., Kalikow, J., Walsh, B. T., Davies, M., Braiman, S., & Dolinsky, A. (1990). "Uncommon troubles in young people: Prevalence estimates of selected psychiatric disorders in a non-referred adolescent population." *Archives of General Psychiatry* 47: 487–496.

White, R. (1974). "Adolescent and pubescent self-disclosure patterns: Phenomenal ratings of the privacy and importance of topics." *Dissertation Abstracts International* 35A(8): 5054.

Whitney, I., & Smith, P. K. (1992). "A survey of the nature and extent of bullying in junior/middle and secondary schools." *Educational Research.*

Wiebe, B., & Scott, T. B. (1976). "Self-disclosure inventory for adolescents." *Psychological Reports* 34: 355–358.

Wiebe, B., & Williams, J. D. (1972). "Self disclosure to parents by high school students." *Psychological Reports* 31: 690.

Wiggins, J. D., & Moody, A. H. (1987). "Student evaluations of counseling programs: An added dimension." *The School Counselor* 34(5): 353–359.

Wilkins, W. (1973). "Expectancy of therapeutic gain: An empirical and conceptual critique." *Journal of Consulting and Clinical Psychology* 40(1): 69–77.

———. (1979). "Expectancies in therapy research: Discriminating among heterogenous non-specifics." *Journal of Consulting and Clinical Psychology* 47(5): 837–859. EJ223360.

Wilks, J. (1986). "The relative importance of parents and friends in adolescent decision-making." *Journal of Youth and Adolescence* 15(4): 323–334.

Williams, C. L., & Uchiyama, C. (1989). "Assessment of life events during adolescence: The use of self report inventories." *Adolescence* 24(93): 95–118.

Wilson, G. T. (1979). "Perceived control and the theory and practice of behaviour therapy." In L. C. Perlmuter & R. A. Monty (Eds.), *Choice and Perceived Control.* Hillsdale, NJ: Erlbaum.

Wilson, M., Robinson, E. J., & Ellis, A. (1989). "Studying communication between community pharmacists and their customers." *Counselling Psychology Quarterly* 2(3): 367–380.

Windle, M. (1994). "A study of friendship characteristics and problem behaviours among middle adolescents." *Child Development* 65: 1764–1777.

Wintre, M. G., Hicks, R., McVey, G., & Fox, J. (1988). "Age and sex differences in choice of consultant for various types of problem." *Child Development* 59: 1046–1055.

Wolcott, I. H. (1986). "Seeking help for marital problems before separation." *Australian Journal of Sex, Marriage, and Family* 7(3): 154–164.

Wolcott, I. H., & Glezer, H. (1989). *Marriage Counselling in Australia: An Evaluation.* Melbourne: Australian Institute of Family Studies. ED325793.

Woods, M., & Melnick, J. (1979). "A review of group therapy selection criteria." *Small Group Behaviour* 10(2): 155–175. EJ200928.

Worthington, E. L. (1986). "Client compliance with homework directives during counseling." *Journal of Counseling Psychology* 33(2): 124–130.

Wright, P. H., & Keple, T. W. (1981). "Friends and parents of a sample of high-school juniors: An exploratory study of relationship intensity and interpersonal rewards." *Journal of Marriage and the Family* 43: 559–570.

Wright, W. (1975). "Relationships of trust and racial perceptions towards therapist–client conditions during counseling." *Journal of Negro Education* 44(2): 161–169. EJ118525.

Yaffe, M. J., & Stewart, M. A. (1986). "Patients' attitudes to the relevance of non-medical problems in family medicine care." *Journal of Family Practice* 23(3): 241–244.

Yalof, J. A. (1987). "Client perceptions of the intake-referral process in a college walk-in clinic: Monitoring the latent content." *Journal of College Student Psychotherapy* 1(3): 59–68.

Yalom, I. (1966). "A study of group therapy dropouts." *Archives of General Psychiatry* 14: 393–414.

Yamamoto, K., Soliman, A., Parsons, J., & Davies, O. L. (1987). "Voices in unison: Stressful events in the lives of children in six countries." *Journal of Child Psychology and Psychiatry* 28(6): 855–864.

Yau, T. Y., & Hayden, D. (1992). "Counseling style preferences of international students." *Journal of Counseling Psychology* 39(1): 100–104.

Young, R. (1989). "Helpful behaviours in the crisis center call." *Journal of Community Psychology* 7(1): 70–77.

Youniss, J., & Ketterlinus, R. D. (1987). "Communication and connectedness in mother–father–adolescent relationships." *Journal of Youth and Adolescence* 16(3): 265–280.

Youniss, J., & Smollar, J. (1985). *Adolescent Relations with Mothers, Fathers, and Friends.* Chicago: University of Chicago Press.

Yuen, R. K., & Tinsley, H.E.A. (1981). "International and American students' gender preferences for counselors." *Journal of Counseling Psychology* 28: 66–69.

Zimmerman-Tansella, C., & Colorio, C. (1986). "Early dropouts' and clients' experience of family therapy." *International Journal of Family Psychiatry* 7(3): 203–220.

Zirkle, G. A. (1961). "Five minute psychotherapy." *American Journal of Psychiatry* 118: 544–546.

Ziv, A., & Shauber, H. (1972). "Sex differences in the life problems and interests of adolescents." *International Journal of Psychology* 7: 33–37.

Zytowski, D. G., Casas, J. M., Gilbert, L. A., Lent, R. W., & Simon, N. P. (1988). "Counseling psychology's public image." *The Counseling Psychologist* 16(3): 322–346.

Name Index

Subject Index

ABOUT THE AUTHOR

Tony Branwhite, Ph.D., is Principal Psychologist with the Directorate of Education and Personal Development at North Lincolnshire Council.